Mini-Lessons
for Teaching About Nonfiction

Teacher-Tested Lessons With Research-Based Strategies That Introduce Key Nonfiction Features and Build Comprehension

DIANE FARNHAM, PAULA JENSVOLD & BRIGID KULHOWVICK

New York • Toronto • London • Auckland • Sydney
Mexico City • New Delhi • Hong Kong • Buenos Aires

Teaching
Resources

*In appreciation of all the children who have traveled with us
on our journey as lifelong learners.*

Edited by Joan Novelli.

Cover design by Brian LaRossa.

Cover photograph © Tim Hall/Getty Images.

Interior design by Holly Grundon.

Interior art by Maxie Chambliss.

Interior photographs copyright © 2007 by Diane Farnham, Paula Jensvold, and Brigid
Kulhowvick, except for pages 3 (center), 42, 77, and 80 © 2007 by Sally Twente Wong,
pages 4 and 7 © D. Vincenzo Novelli, and pages 16 and 58 © by Holly Grundon.

ISBN-13: 978-0-439-85656-0

ISBN-10: 0-439-85656-6

Copyright © 2007 by Diane Farnham, Paula Jensvold, and Brigid Kulhowvick.

Contents

From the Authors

Change can be unsettling, but sometimes it is change that leads us to open new doors and make new connections. We were faced with this opportunity when restructuring occurred in our district. Through new classroom assignments, we found ourselves teaching in the same building for the first time. We began the year teaching beside each other and grew to teach with each other.

This book evolved out of our shared belief that young children need opportunities to experience and explore nonfiction. Traditionally in primary grades, literacy instruction revolves around fiction. Our shared vision was to provide our students with supported opportunities to interact with nonfiction so that it became as natural as reading fiction.

As we began our teaching of nonfiction, our students became our teachers. It was through their eyes that we were inspired to design, share, and adapt the collaborative work of this book.

Just as we've enjoyed our journey of learning together, we now invite you to use these ideas and make them your own as you and your colleagues open new doors to the world of nonfiction for young learners.

—Diane Farnham, Paula Jensvold, and Brigid Kulhowvick

About This Book

A first grader burst through the classroom door one September morning carrying a treasure in a jar. "Look what I found last night! It's a monarch caterpillar." We all gathered around the jar to examine the tiny creature within. As we watched the caterpillar over the next several weeks, we saw it grow and change into a chrysalis. One day during morning meeting, one of the children noticed that the chrysalis, now a transparent covering over the butterfly growing within, was starting to crack open. Carefully, I set the jar down in the middle of our circle. Lying close together on our stomachs, we held our breath and watched the miracle of a monarch butterfly emerge. As my students and I watched with wonder, I couldn't help but think that teaching and learning are much like the metamorphosis of a monarch. As teachers, we guide our students through many changes so that, one day, they can emerge and fly off into the world. Seeing children's faces light up when they learn something new is as miraculous as witnessing a butterfly take flight for the first time.

What the Research Says About Teaching Nonfiction

Young children are filled with wonder. They want to know how the world works and what their place is in it. It's a child's natural curiosity in the world around him that is supported through reading nonfiction. The research is clear: Young children can interact successfully with informational text. (Dreher, 2000; Duke, 2003; and Duke, Bennett-Armistead, and Roberts, 2002; 2003; as cited in Duke and Bennett-Armistead, 2003)* Children can learn to read at the same time they are reading to learn!

Often because of the challenging vocabulary in nonfiction, books in this genre are reserved for use in upper elementary grades. We expect our fourth- and fifth-grade students to begin to use reading more as a way to obtain information. They are now "reading to learn rather than learning to read." (Chall, 1983; as cited in Duke and Bennett-Armistead, 2003) Standardized tests often require a student to read a nonfiction passage and answer questions. But when do we teach them how to read nonfiction? It is important that young learners have experiences with nonfiction text so that later they can access this text with ease. The many features of nonfiction that can make it difficult to follow are also the same features that can instantly pique a young reader's curiosity— colorful pictures, bold titles, diagrams, maps, and captions. These can provide young readers with a unique motivation and natural engagement, which is essential to the reading process. (Gambrell, 1996; Guthrie and Wigfield, 2000; as cited in Duke and Bennett-Armistead, 2003) Additionally, the fact that information can be acquired from any part of the book without necessarily having to follow the sequence of beginning, middle, and end is very freeing to many young readers.

When primary teachers understand what their students will encounter in later grades, they can lay the foundation that supports that learning. The nonfiction reading and writing that happens in primary classrooms does not and should not mirror the kinds of reading and writing going on in the upper elementary grades. Just as the caterpillar needs to eat and eat and eat before transforming into a chrysalis and then a butterfly, the primary classroom provides our young readers with the nourishment that will sustain them later.

Teaching Tip

Research conducted with kindergartners and second graders found that children can engage in research with text when they are given support.

(Korkeamaki and Dreher, 2000; Korkeamaki, Tiainen, and Dreher, 1998; as cited in Duke and Bennett-Armistead, 2003)

How to Use This Book

With ongoing exposure to nonfiction materials, students will naturally become experienced with accessing facts and information to help them become experts on a topic. You can easily embed intentional teaching of nonfiction features in your yearlong literacy program to enhance students' overall literacy skills. There are different approaches you can take with the lessons in this book to accomplish this goal.

* Duke, N. K. and Bennett-Armistead, V. S. (2003). *Reading & writing informational text in the primary grades: Research-based practices.* New York: Scholastic.

Teaching Features of Nonfiction as a Unit of Study: You may use the lessons in this book to teach features as part of a cohesive unit of study. You might then culminate students' knowledge by having each student create a "Features of Nonfiction" reference book, or compile one as a class, adding pages with each new lesson. (See "Your Students as Researchers and Writers," page 84.)

Teaching Features of Nonfiction in Conjunction With Research Projects: Researching with young learners provides many meaningful opportunities to teach and revisit the various features of nonfiction. For example, students may undertake research to explore a science topic or investigate an interest. It is important for you to understand your desired outcomes before you proceed much further with your students. Focusing on the product of the research is the immediate goal. By including supports for all levels of learning, you also enable students to spend time gathering information, building information webs, organizing facts, and becoming "experts" on a given topic. Through this process students naturally build reading and writing skills. (Schiefele, Krapp, and Winteler, 1992; as cited in Duke and Bennett-Armistead, 2003) Use the materials in this book in any order to teach whole-class or small-group lessons on features of nonfiction as various opportunities arise.

Teaching Tip

It is also valuable to consider using the process of research as the focus for young learners. Identifying and following the steps of research—choosing topics of interest, selecting appropriate resources, accessing the information, organizing it, and sharing it—are in themselves literacy tools for young learners. Confidence as a researcher grows out of becoming a self-reliant learner.

Lesson Components

Chapters 1–9: Each lesson provides a complete framework for teaching a key feature or structure of nonfiction. From scripted dialogue you can use as a model to introduce the lesson to a list of nonfiction books that support each lesson, here's what you'll find:

Section	Description
Introduce	This section of the lesson is presented in an easy-to-adapt scripted format to provide you with a teacher-tested approach for introducing the target nonfiction feature and engaging students in more effective learning.
Explore and Discover	Use the ideas here to scaffold students' experiences in identifying and using the various features of nonfiction.
Share and Discuss	Review each nonfiction feature with ideas that let students interact with each other and create displays that highlight what they've learned.
Need More Practice?	Use these suggestions to provide further instruction on the topic with individuals, small groups, or the whole class.
Reading-Writing Connections	Students connect what they do as readers to what they do as writers with these lesson extensions. Often these lessons work well as informal assessment.
Teaching Connections and Extensions	Integrate nonfiction features with other content strands, and explore opportunities to develop additional literacy skills.
Nonfiction Books to Use With This Lesson	An annotated book list for each lesson suggests nonfiction children's books that provide especially good examples of the targeted nonfiction feature. These lists also correlate with favorite classroom themes. For example, if you're teaching about insects, you'll find books that are just right for that.
Teaching Tips	These tips provide additional support and include professional development tips, suggestions for adapting activities to individual needs, classroom management strategies, and more.
Reproducible Pages	These ready-to-use graphic organizers, record sheets, and templates assist students in recording and applying what they learn.

Chapter 10: This chapter introduces four additional features of nonfiction and provides mini-lessons for teaching them within the context of a larger lesson, or as opportunities arise. With these mini-lessons, children explore titles and how they relate to topics and main ideas, print styles and how they may connect to a book's content, sidebars and how authors use them to introduce new information, and opening and closing sentences as they relate to the organizing framework in a nonfiction text.

Chapter 11: As a culminating activity, use the ideas in this section to create books that combine what students are learning in an area of study (such as social studies or science) with what they are learning about features of nonfiction. A mini-lesson on paraphrasing helps students understand the importance of putting information in their own words.

Connections to the Language Arts Standards

The lessons in this book are designed to support you in meeting the following language arts standards as outlined by Mid-continent Research for Education and Learning (McREL), an organization that collects and synthesizes national and state K–12 curriculum standards.

Reading

❊ Uses reading skills and strategies to understand a variety of informational texts.

❊ Uses mental images based on pictures and print to aid in comprehension of text.

❊ Uses meaning clues to aid comprehension and make predictions about content.

❊ Understands level-appropriate sight words and vocabulary.

❊ Understands the main idea and supporting details of simple expository information.

❊ Makes contributions in class and group discussions.

❊ Asks and responds to questions.

❊ Summarizes information found in texts.

❊ Relates new information to prior knowledge and experience.

Writing

❊ Writes (or uses emergent writing) in a variety of forms or genres and for different purposes.

❊ Uses writing and other methods to describe familiar persons, places, objects, or experiences.

❊ Generates questions about topics of personal interest.

❊ Gathers and uses information for research purposes.

❊ Uses strategies to compile information into written reports or summaries (for example, incorporates notes; includes facts, details, explanations, and examples; uses diagrams or other visual aids).

Source: Kendall, J. S. and Marzano, R. J. (2004). *Content knowledge: A compendium of standards and benchmarks for K–12 education.* Aurora, CO: Mid-continent Research for Education and Learning. Online database: http://www.mcrel.org/standards-benchmarks.

Chapter One

Getting Started With Nonfiction

I sat with a basket of books balanced on my knees. The basket, which we labeled earlier in the year, reads "Fantasy." "If you were choosing a book from this basket, what kind of book might you expect to find?" I ask a curious group of first and second graders. "Storybooks," "picture books," "fantasy books," and "books that are make-believe" are some of the responses I get. I pick up one of the books for all to see. "What if I choose this book to read?" I read the title and author, The Gingerbread Baby by Jan Brett. "What are some things you would find in this book?" My students know the book well and are eager to respond. They are very familiar with fiction.

"Today we are going to begin learning about another type of book." I have collected an assortment of nonfiction books, which I have loaded into a red wagon. I wheel the wagon into the middle of our circle. The children are immediately excited because all the books are hardcover and rather thick looking, very much like books that only a "good reader" would use. Suddenly, the children are on their knees, leaning in, eager to touch the treasures in front of them.

Introduce: What Is Nonfiction?

Lead students through a brief introduction to nonfiction, using the script below as a guide. Then provide time for children to discover and explore nonfiction books they choose. They may spend time reading a favorite, focus on particular pages, or take a "picture walk" through several to see what interests them most. (See Explore and Discover, below.) Then bring students together to share. (See Share and Discuss, page 12.) The sample dialogue provided gives you an idea of what to expect: Students will be eager to share fascinating details and comments about the books they've just explored.

"What about these books?" I ask, as I pull several out of the wagon and place them in our circle.

"They're about real stuff!" exclaims Will.

"They probably have facts in them," adds Rachel.

"That one's about dinosaurs. Can I have that one?" Connor can't wait to get his hands on the book.

"They're nonfiction," declares Alex.

"That's right," I say. "These books are called nonfiction books. We've been reading lots and lots of storybooks." [I point to the fantasy basket.] "You know a lot about reading fiction. You know about characters, problems, and solutions. You know about stories having a beginning, middle, and end. Today I'd like you to choose nonfiction books to read."

Teaching Tip

Just as it is important to give children time to explore new math materials, they also need time to browse and explore new genres of literature. Before introducing formal lessons on features of nonfiction, give children time to dive in and see what they can discover about nonfiction on their own.

Explore and Discover

My direction is simple: "While you read, think about what's special about nonfiction. We'll share our discoveries at the end of our reading time."

Children can hardly wait to get started, and the classroom quickly becomes abuzz with "Ooohs!" and "Aaahs!" and "Wow! Look at this!" Soon there are clusters of students reading together and talking about the neat things they are learning.

As students select and explore nonfiction books from the class collection, circulate among them and ask questions to guide their discoveries:

❊ Why do you think the author wrote this book? What do you think you might learn by reading this book?

❊ How do you think the author gathered information to write this book about [topic]? What resources do you use to get information about topics you're interested in?

❊ How is this book like other books you've read? How is it different?

As we regroup, the sharing is animated. My students are eager to share the information they learned.

"Did you know there is a jellyfish that is about three times as big as a man?" William says, holding up a diagram he found while reading about the ocean.

"I found a T. rex," reports Mark.

"And I found frogs that were all different colors!" adds Emma.

It is clear that children's curiosity is captured by the information in the books. They have already experienced success—skipping over sections that don't interest them or make sense to connect with random facts of interest. The feeling of power that comes from being able to access information has already begun to build each child's confidence as a reader.

"Wow, you learned a lot today while you were reading!" I pause, then continue, *"I'm wondering something. Why do you think people read nonfiction?"*

"To learn new things," they respond.

"And why do people read fiction?" I wonder aloud.

"I read fiction because it's fun to read a story, and I read nonfiction to learn new stuff. That's fun, too!" says Caroline.

I have set the stage for a comparison of fiction and nonfiction. We spend the next few days becoming familiar with nonfiction books. My role during this time is to help children notice features as they arise. One way to do this is to use a Venn diagram to compare and contrast fiction and nonfiction. (See Reading-Writing Connections, page 13.)

Children enjoy sorting and classifying, and this is one way to provide further practice in identifying characteristics of nonfiction texts. Place an assortment of fiction and nonfiction books in baskets. Invite children to work with partners or in small groups to sort them, using what they know about both genres to place the books in two groups: Fiction and Nonfiction. As children classify the books, encourage them to compare features of fiction and nonfiction. What are some clues that a book is fiction? For example, as children flip through pages of a book, they might notice the illustrations and ask themselves, "Could this really happen?" To go further, students can classify nonfiction books into categories such as informational, how-to, "true stories," and biographies.

Using a Venn Diagram

Review with students that they have been making discoveries about the many features of nonfiction. Then help them make connections to other genres they know by using a Venn diagram to compare nonfiction with fiction. Point out that students might notice Venn diagrams and other graphic aids in books they read. Explain that these tools help readers visualize information. Today, tell them, they will create a Venn diagram to show how fiction and nonfiction are alike and different. Let students know they can use Venn diagrams and other visual aids in their own writing to help readers make sense of information. (For more on teaching about graphic aids in nonfiction, see pages 26, 34, 42, 50, and 64.)

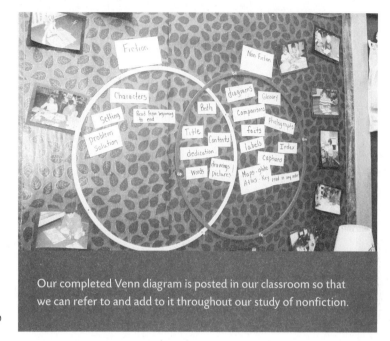

Our completed Venn diagram is posted in our classroom so that we can refer to and add to it throughout our study of nonfiction.

1. Set up a Venn diagram to illustrate the differences and similarities between fiction and nonfiction. To begin, draw two large intersecting circles (see sample, above).

2. Tell students: *You have been reading and making discoveries about nonfiction books. Today we are going to create a Venn diagram to compare fiction and nonfiction.* (You may want to make a connection to previous Venn diagrams students have created.)

3. Label the Venn diagram with students. As you point to the circle on the left, explain: *This circle represents fiction.* Label the circle "Fiction." Repeat for the circle on the right, labeling it "Nonfiction."

4. Ask students what they think the area where the circles overlap represents. Label the area "Both," and review that it represents what fiction and nonfiction have in common.

5. To complete the Venn diagram, ask: *What are some things that you know about fiction and nonfiction that are different or the same?*

Teaching Tip

Use one color for fiction and a different color for nonfiction. This clearly shows children that the circles represent two different types of books.

Responses may include: "Fiction is not true and nonfiction is true." "Fiction is a story." "Fiction has a beginning, middle, and end. You can read nonfiction in any order." "Both have an author." "Both have a title." The list goes on and on. Record responses in the appropriate areas of the Venn diagram.

6. Display the Venn diagram and review with students that presenting the facts this way (as opposed to in paragraph form) helps readers more easily make sense of the information.

Teaching Connections and Extensions

Students may be surprised at the many places they can find nonfiction. Invite them to look around the room for examples. They may find it in books on shelves and in baskets, in charts and graphs on the walls, in newspapers on your desk, on a map posted by the door, in instructions for games, in their science textbooks, on the Internet, and elsewhere. Take opportunities to make connections to nonfiction in daily activities—for example:

❈ in science, as children read and follow steps for conducting an experiment or analyze data on a weather graph.

❈ in social studies, as children read and learn about people, places, and their environment.

❈ in physical education, as children review posters on the wall about healthy habits.

❈ in math, as children read explanations about how to solve a problem.

❈ in print around the room that informs students of the daily schedule, reminds them of class expectations, charts reading strategies, and so on.

Nonfiction Books to Use With This Lesson

To introduce a study of features of nonfiction, gather any collection of nonfiction that you think will capture your students' interest. Following are a few suggestions, each of which also offers young readers an introduction to the particular features of nonfiction covered in this book.

Amazing Animal Facts by Jacqui Bailey, Joe Elliot, and Jayne Miller (Dorling Kindersley, 2003): This popular classroom resource combines fascinating facts with photographs to engage and inform young readers.

Biggest, Strongest, Fastest by Steve Jenkins (Ticknor & Fields, 1995): From a tiny flea to the mammoth blue whale, this book of records invites children to compare and contrast animals' characteristics to their own.

Houses and Homes **(Around the World Series)** by Ann Morris (Lothrop, Lee and Shepard, 1992): Vibrant full-color photos take readers around the world to see how people in different places live.

Martin's Big Words by Doreen Rappaport (Hyperion, 2001): This Caldecott Honor pictorial biography of Dr. Martin Luther King's life features a time line of important dates.

The Post Office Book: Mail and How It Moves by Gail Gibbons (Thomas Y. Crowell, 1982): Follow a letter from the time it is dropped in a mailbox until it reaches its destination.

Tell Me Tree: All About Trees for Kids by Gail Gibbons (Little, Brown, 2002): Vivid illustrations and labels help young readers learn how to identify trees.

This Land Is Your Land by Woody Guthrie (Little, Brown, 1998): Students may find themselves singing along to the familiar lyrics as they learn about America's history and geography.

Throw Your Tooth on the Roof: Tooth Traditions From Around the World by Selby Beeler (Houghton Mifflin, 2001): Explore traditions around the world with a playful look at what happens when children lose their teeth.

Waiting for Wings by Lois Ehlert (Harcourt, 2001): "Out in the fields, eggs are hidden from view, clinging to leaves with butterfly glue." A favorite feature of this book is the mini-book within the book that tells the story of caterpillars. Pages grow in size as the butterflies emerge.

Wake Up World! A Day in the Life of Children Around the World by Beatrice Hollyer (Henry Holt, 1999): The author compares and contrasts to take readers through a typical day in the lives of children around the world. A large map lets readers locate where each child lives.

Chapter Two

Contents Page and Index

A fter being in school for a couple of months, children have become very accustomed to following our daily schedule that is posted on the board each day. Today, before children arrive, I remove our schedule cards. Within the first ten minutes of the day, I begin to get reminders and questions.

"Mrs. Farnham, you forgot to put up the schedule!"

"Mrs. Farnham, there's no schedule. How are we going to know what comes next?"

The stage for our literacy-time topic has been set! In the same way that children rely on the daily schedule to make sense of their day and locate information, they learn that books have a contents page and index to show how they're organized.

A contents page is the first feature of organization that readers encounter. It lists all the main topics of a book and tells readers where to locate information in the book. A contents page gives readers an overall sense of what the text includes and how the author has chosen to organize the information. Readers can use the contents page to make predictions about a nonfiction book. The scripted lesson that follows is based on *Getting to Know Nature's Children: Chipmunks*, by Merebeth Switzer (Grolier, 1985), but you can easily substitute another nonfiction title and modify the dialogue accordingly.

Teacher: *When you come into the classroom each day, you can check the daily schedule to see what our plans are for the day. Today some of you noticed our schedule was missing. We didn't know what to expect! When we can see how our day is organized, it helps us know what to expect and predict how the day will go. Books have ways of being organized as well. We've been reading a lot of storybooks and also a lot of chapter books. What is the difference between the two? Why do you think the chapter book has chapters? Do you think all thick books have chapters? Do you think any thin books have chapters?*

Today I've chosen a nonfiction book for us to read together, Getting to Know Nature's Children: Chipmunks, *by Merebeth Switzer. What do you predict it will be about? Do you think it will have chapters? Let's open it and see.*

This is the contents page. It tells us what we can expect to read about in this book. Listen to the names of some of the chapters and think about which chapter sounds most interesting to you.

> *"What a Chipmunk Looks Like Up Close"*
>
> *"How a Chipmunk Takes a Bath"*
>
> *"What Chipmunks Like to Eat"*
>
> *"What Baby Chipmunks Look Like"*

One fun thing about reading nonfiction books is that you don't necessarily have to read the chapters in order from beginning to end! The contents page is a great tool for helping you decide where you might best look for the reading that is going to be most interesting and useful to you. For example, if I wanted to find out about what a chipmunk eats, I can use the contents page to figure out the best place to begin reading: page 25. I don't have to read every page before that because I can tell which chapter has the information I need.

Let's try another one. This chapter sounds interesting to me: "When Chipmunks Go to Bed." I wonder if it will tell me what time they go to bed or what their bed is like. If I want to find out, I can just turn to page 44 and read this chapter. [This book has short chapters so I read it aloud to the class. We find all the answers to our questions. Now we're ready for more!]

Explore and Discover

Explain to students that now it's their turn to use the contents page in a book they choose. Remind them that with nonfiction, they don't have to start reading right at the beginning of the book.

Teacher: *Today I want you to make a thoughtful choice about where to start reading your book by using the contents page. Choose a book from our collection and find the contents page. Then choose a chapter that seems interesting to you and begin reading there. When you're finished with that chapter, go back to the contents page and choose another interesting chapter. As you explore, you may use a sticky note to mark a particularly interesting chapter that you might want to share with the class when we gather on the rug.*

Introduce: What Is an Index?

An index is an alphabetical list of topics included in a nonfiction book. It is located at the end of a book and tells which pages contain information about each topic. An index helps readers locate information quickly—without reading the entire book. The scripted lesson that follows is based on *Exploring the World of Animals*, by Penny Raife Durant (Franklin Watts, 1985), but you can easily substitute another nonfiction title and modify the dialogue accordingly.

Teacher: *There's another organizing feature in nonfiction books that also helps readers locate information. It is called the index. Most, but not all, nonfiction books have an index. Does anyone know where to find the index? That's right—it's at the very back of the book. Let's look for the index in this book,* Exploring the World of Animals, *by Penny Raife Durant. Here it is on the very last page of the book! The title on this page even says "Index."* [Show students the index page.]

The index lists all the important subjects included in the book. What do you know about the word subject? [Invite responses.] *The word* subject *is another word for* topic, *or* idea. *A subject might be the name of a person, place, or thing.*

	Let's take a closer look at this index. It's a long list. Let me show you the first five subjects listed in this index. [I write the first five subjects on the board: Abdomen, Adaptation, Air, Baleen, Beak.] *What do you notice?*
Child:	*I see that the first three words all start with A and then the next two start with B. Probably the next one will start with B or C.*
Teacher:	*You've got it! The first ones start with A, the next group starts with B, and you're right about C coming next. This is called...*
Child:	*I know, alphabetical order! All the words are written down in the same order as the alphabet.*
Teacher:	*That's right. Why do you suppose the author chose to list these topics in alphabetical order?*
Child:	*I think it's because it keeps them all organized. So then if you're trying to find one, you can easily figure out where it is.*
Teacher:	*Good thinking! Look at the other information the author gives us.* [List the page numbers after each topic.] *These numbers are the page numbers where you would find information on that topic. Why do you think there is more than one page number?*
Child:	*There's probably information about it on more than one page in the book, so it tells you all the pages to look on.*
Teacher:	*That's right. When I look carefully, I notice that some page numbers are written in a different kind of print. It looks kind of slanted and is called italics. This is a signal that the page numbers written in italics will have a picture. Let's see if that's true.* [The numeral 7 after Gorilla is written in italics, so we check on page 7 and sure enough there is a full-page picture of a gorilla, along with a caption that gives us additional information—and a chance to preview another feature of nonfiction.]
	Sometimes authors use bold or dark print instead of italics to show the pages that have pictures. In our book today there is a sentence right here at the top of the index that reminds us of the author's choice to put the numbers in italics to show illustrations. Now it's time for you to explore our books and use the index.

Explore and Discover

Provide time for students to continue to browse their nonfiction books and practice locating and using the index. As students use the index of their books to locate information on specific topics, remind them to keep the following in mind:

❋ Look for the index in the back of the book. If the book you choose doesn't have an index, please exchange it for another one that does.

* Read through the list of subjects.

* Choose one that interests you, check the page number, and then find it in the book and read about it.

* Use a sticky note to mark a particularly interesting fact or picture that you find and would like to share later with the group.

Share and Discuss

Invite children to share how they will use the contents page and index in their own reading. Ask: *How can reading a contents page help you know if you're interested in reading the book? How can using an index help you know if a book has enough information on the topic you want to learn about?*

Have students work in small groups to create wall charts or displays that highlight what they've learned about using a contents page and index. These visual aids will serve as reminders to children as they apply what they've learned in their independent reading.

Contents Page	Index
* Found in the beginning of the book.	* Found at the end of the book.
* Lists chapter titles.	* Lists key subjects in the book.
* Organizes the big ideas of the book.	* Subjects are listed in ABC order.
* Shows the beginning page number of each chapter.	* Subtopics may be listed beneath main subjects.
	* More than one page number may be listed after each subject.
	* Page numbers written in italics or bold print indicate which pages have pictures.

Need More Practice?

Use the reproducible Detective Log (page 24) to provide students with extra practice in locating both the contents page and the index in a book. For books with a contents page, have students preview the contents page for a chapter that looks especially interesting to them. Encourage them to notice how books with a contents page and an index make it easier to locate specific information.

Researching and Taking Notes

After finding an appropriate book, a researcher must then determine how best to use the book as a resource. Young readers will usually flip through the pages looking for engaging illustrations. Provide practice in using the contents page and index to strengthen specific skills that enable children to make thoughtful decisions about how to use a book in a more organized and helpful way.

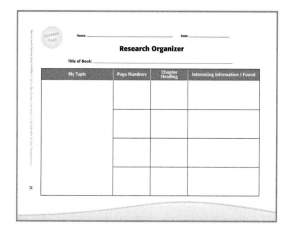

1. Before students research on their own, model your thought process in locating the information you need, incorporating both the contents page and index in the discussion:

    I am very interested in different endangered animals and would like to do some research on a particular one, but I'm not sure which one to choose. As I look in the index of my book Endangered Animals, *I notice lots of possibilities. I wonder if it would be more helpful for me to choose an animal that has a lot of page numbers after it, or one that has only one page number.*

2. Guide children to recognize that many page numbers after an entry probably means that the book has lots of information about that topic, which would be helpful to the researcher.

3. Further model your thought processes around how you decide which of the page numbers in the index are likely to correspond to pages of interest to you. Demonstrate how you can use the contents page to learn more about this. Begin by choosing a topic, such as "Eagles," that is of interest and has at least a couple of page numbers listed in the index. (Avoid, at this point, going beyond ten page numbers for a topic.) Introduce the Research Organizer (page 25) before you begin, and model how to use it as you continue.

    I wonder which chapters these pages go with. Knowing that will help me understand what the author wants me to learn about eagles before I start reading. [Check the contents page and read and record the titles of the corresponding chapters. Read a section related to your topic, and record a piece of interesting information on the organizer.]

4. Give each student a copy of the Research Organizer. Ask students to choose a topic or subject in the index of their book that interests them and also has lots of information. Have students complete the organizer for that topic. For additional practice, they may move on to another subject that interests them in that same book or in a different book (using a fresh organizer).

Teaching Connections and Extensions

There's a treasure hunt-like appeal to a contents page and index that offers children intrinsic rewards when they find what they're looking for. While the contents page might tell them a book contains information about zebras, the index will reveal on what pages they can more specifically learn about different species of zebras, their habitat, diet, predators, stripe patterns, and more. For students who are investigating areas of interest, this is an exciting discovery. Students will also discover that these features are time-savers for readers. Try these ideas to help children make connections between what they're learning about these features of nonfiction and how they can use that knowledge in other activities.

* Invite students to preview the contents page of a nonfiction book you're reading in a content area to get an idea of what information the book covers. Does the contents page tell them the book also has an index? Check that out, too, to see how much detail is provided on favorite topics. For practice, try naming a topic and challenging children to use the contents page or index to find the page number.

* Connect phonics lessons on alphabetical order with the alphabetizing skills children need to use an index as a reading tool. Write each child's name on a 3- by 5-inch index card. Have children work in groups to alphabetize the cards. Guide children as necessary in understanding how to alphabetize names that begin with the same letter (go to the second and third letter). As they use nonfiction books throughout the day—for example, in math— encourage them to notice the order of words in the index, and what happens when there is more than one entry for a letter (such as *Giraffe, Goat, Grizzly Bear*).

* To go further, consider having students each write a page for a class book about a topic the class is studying (such as Baby Animals), and then work together to create a contents page and index for the book.

Teaching Tip

Throughout the course of the year, it is very powerful for students to have the opportunity to pursue personal-interest research. The lessons and practice on using a contents page and index are invaluable in getting young researchers started on a successful and organized path. Use the Research Organizer (page 25) with these personal-interest research projects to help students organize information as they research their topics. The chart will assist them later as they organize their writing.

Nonfiction Books to Use With This Lesson

Each of the following titles is just right for teaching young readers how to use a contents page and index.

The Best Book of Bugs by Claire Llewellyn (Kingfisher Publications, 1998): As children flip from the contents page to the glossary, they will feel as if they are stepping into the world of some of the weirdest and most wonderful insect creatures! Realistic artwork and specific scientific language helps little readers become big scientists.

Endangered Animals by Lynn M. Stone (Children's Press, 1984): This extensive collection of photographs features many endangered animals that are appealing to young children. Large print, a simple contents page, and a substantial index make this book especially user-friendly for young researchers.

Getting to Know Nature's Children by Merebeth Switzer (Grolier, 1985): Part of a series of fascinating nature books, this selection offers a wealth of information on topics most appealing to young children—animals! Short chapters combine with a complete, yet not overwhelming, index to provide a successful first step into research.

Piglets by Kelly Doudna (ABDO Publishing, 1999): Inviting pictures and simple sentences draw in beginning readers. This is one of six books in the Baby Animals series. Well-constructed support features, such as a simple contents page, index, and glossary, provide the perfect tools for young researchers to hone their skills.

Thunderstorms and Lightning by Dean Galiano (Rosen Publishing Group, 2003): What is more captivating to young children than the excitement of thunder and lightning! This book is full of information about the science of electrical storms as well as appropriate safety measures for children to know.

Usborne Internet-Linked First Encyclopedia of the Human Body by Fiona Chandler (Usborne, 2004): An abundance of information is organized in a very accessible way for young researchers as they begin to appreciate the use of an encyclopedia as a resource.

Where Did the Butterfly Get Its Name? by Melvin and Gilda Berger (Scholastic, 2003): A wealth of information with lifelike illustrations follows an easy-to-access format of questions and answers. This title is sure to pique the curiosity of young researchers.

Teaching Tip

If you're teaching with themes, these selections include the following topics: insects, endangered animals, baby animals, farm animals, weather, and the human body. Incorporating lessons on features of nonfiction with topics children are exploring provides meaningful practice and deepens understanding. For more thematic connections to nonfiction children's books, see the chart on pages 90–91.

Name: _____ Date: _____

Detective Log: Contents Page and Index

Books	Contents Page?	Index?	Interesting Chapter
Book Title: _____	_____ Yes _____ No	_____ Yes _____ No	Chapter Title: _____
Book Title: _____	_____ Yes _____ No	_____ Yes _____ No	Chapter Title: _____
Book Title: _____	_____ Yes _____ No	_____ Yes _____ No	Chapter Title: _____
Book Title: _____	_____ Yes _____ No	_____ Yes _____ No	Chapter Title: _____

Name: _____

Date: _____

Research Organizer

Title of Book: _____

My Topic	Page Numbers	Chapter Heading	

Chapter Three

Diagrams

It was early in October when Sam (a very emergent reader) approached me with a nonfiction book and said, "Look! I found a picture of a cat." He proceeded to point to and read almost all the labels on the page. I let him know that this was a good book choice and suggested he continue to read this book silently during our reading time.

After silent reading time, Sam proudly carried the book to our circle and quickly raised his hand to share that today he had found a book in the classroom that he could read. The other children (all excited for Sam) responded with questions and comments. Sam was able to articulately answer the questions and show the other children where he found the book. The next day, during silent reading time, the nonfiction basket of science books was a big hit.

After reflecting on the day, I realized that Sam is a very typical first-grade student. I thought about his writing and realized that many of his journal entries were detailed pictures with labels of people and surrounding objects. It makes sense that children are determined to read exactly how they first learn to write.

A diagram is a special picture that gives the reader information about a topic. It helps the reader to understand difficult information. Labels are words or groups of words that define specific parts of a diagram. Use the scripted lesson that follows first to review with students what they know about characteristics of nonfiction and then to introduce a new feature. This lesson is based on the book *Monarch Butterfly*, by Gail Gibbons (Holiday House, 1989), but you can substitute another nonfiction book and modify the lesson accordingly.

Teacher: *Today I am going to share a nonfiction book with you. Over the past weeks we have read a lot of stories from our fantasy basket. Today I have chosen a book from our science basket. Who can remember one characteristic of a fiction book? Who can remember a characteristic of a nonfiction book?* [Revisit the Venn diagram comparing fiction and nonfiction; see page 13. Add to it if children have new ideas.]

Last night I was thinking about the chrysalis that we have in our classroom. I was trying to remember and get ready to teach you the three main parts of a butterfly. I wrote my question on this index card: What are the three main parts of a butterfly?

I was wondering if this book, Monarch Butterfly, *by Gail Gibbons, will help me find the answer to my question. What do you think? Where do you think is a good place to begin looking?* [Elicit suggestions about looking for a contents page or index. This is a good opportunity to let children know what to do if these features are not present in a book.]

Teaching Tip

You may also use the Research Organizer (page 25) to record information on your topic.

Since there is no contents page or index, I am going to take a picture walk through the book and scan the pages until I get to a page that looks as if it might tell me about the parts of a butterfly.

Do you see this? [Point to the diagram of a butterfly on page 14.] *This is called a diagram. A diagram is a type of picture that gives a reader specific information about a topic. A diagram usually has labels that identify or explain key parts. Do you see anything on this diagram that could help me answer my question?* [Elicit from children that lines from the labels point to parts of the butterfly.]

You helped me find the answer to my question! Watch as I record the information. I'm going to write it on this card [show students an index card], *along with the title of the book and page number in case I need to go back and look for more information or recheck this information.*

Let children know that now it's time for them to explore nonfiction books to find diagrams.

1. In advance, prepare question cards that students will use to investigate different nonfiction books and resources. You can use the cards on pages 32–33 or create your own. Make sure that you have the proper books to support the questions you choose for your students.

2. Give each pair of students a question card. Review with them where they might look to find the answer to their question. Remind students to think about which book may have an appropriate diagram to answer their question, and to use what they've learned about the contents page and index to locate the information.

3. Have students record the answer to the question, along with the title of the book and the page number where they found the diagram and answer.

Share and Discuss

When students have found what they're looking for, bring them together in a circle. Say: *I noticed that many of you were successful in answering your questions today. Would anyone like to share your question and where you found the answer? What was helpful about the diagrams that you found? What did you notice about the diagrams in your book?*

By now students have had several experiences with diagrams to draw upon. They've watched you model finding and using a diagram, and they've explored and shared diagrams they've found themselves. Help students pull together what they've learned: *The past few days you were all successful in locating information to answer the questions that I gave you. Remind me about what you've learned by telling me some things you noticed about the diagrams you found.*

Brainstorm characteristics of diagrams and record students' ideas on chart paper. Let children work together to turn the list of information into a poster they can display in the classroom. Remind them to use the poster as a helpful guide for how to use (and make) diagrams. Ideas might include:

❖ Diagrams have a title.

❖ A diagram is a drawing.

❖ A diagram can have an introduction—a few sentences that tell something about the topic.

❖ Diagrams use labels to tell about important parts.

❖ Boldfaced type highlights important words related to the topic.

❖ Diagrams illustrate information that is in the text.

Have children create questions from diagrams they find. Place these questions in a box. Have students work in pairs or independently to select a question and locate the answer.

Making Diagrams

Help children make a connection between what they do as readers and what they do as writers, using diagrams they see in books as models for creating labeled drawings to illustrate important information in their own writing.

1. Explain to students that they are going to make their own diagrams:

   Today we are going to make our own diagrams. Let's first make a draft and then tomorrow we will publish our diagrams. What do you need to think about when you make your draft? [Remind students that the poster has helpful information about diagrams on it. See Share and Discuss, page 28.]

2. Discuss with students considerations such as the size of the diagram, leaving room for labels, using a pencil first, using a ruler, adding a title, and using a book to help with content-specific words (for labels).

3. Model how to make a diagram, beginning with writing a title at the top of the paper. Include a brief introduction (students might like to know that this is sometimes called a deck) to tell what the diagram is about. Then create the diagram, adding labels that include content-specific vocabulary and using "boldfaced type" as applicable. If you are diagramming a process such as photosynthesis, be sure to number the labeled steps in order. This is a lot for young children to remember, so you may want to chart key points, including:

   ❋ Choose a subject.

   ❋ Research the subject.

   ❋ Use a pencil to make an outline.

   ❋ Add detail and color.

   ❋ Label important parts.

   ❋ Add a title.

4. Have students create a diagram for a topic of interest. This might go with a piece of writing they are working on, a topic they are researching, or an interest they've simply been exploring with nonfiction books. Encourage students to use the poster as a reference to make sure they include the important parts of a diagram. After students create and publish their diagrams, have them share with a neighboring classmate.

Teaching Connections and Extensions

Don't forget that many nonfiction lessons also naturally include an abundance of literacy skills. Making diagrams encourages children to scan information, ask and answer questions, and choose appropriate vocabulary. While students make diagrams, it is a perfect time to discuss the organization of information and the importance of presentation while producing a final product that will be shared with an audience.

This lesson can easily be connected to the morning message as a general assessment or an opportunity for more

This morning message is an example of an intentional connection to a teaching point.

practice. On any given day, simply incorporate into the morning message a diagram of a familiar object without labels. Ask each child to add one label. (If the number of students exceeds the number of possible labels, repeat with new diagrams over several days to give all students a chance.) Look to content area topics of study for diagram subjects—for example:

❖ parts of a fire truck

❖ parts of the human body

❖ parts of a castle

❖ parts of a space shuttle or astronaut's suit

Nonfiction Books to Use With This Lesson

Each of the following titles is just right for teaching young readers how to use a diagram.

Bugs by Nancy Winslow Parker and Joan Richards (Mulberry, 1987): No bug lover should be without this book! *Bugs* is a perfect beginner encyclopedia that introduces 16 familiar insects through the use of scientific drawings and diagrams.

Can It Rain Cats and Dogs? by Melvin and Gilda Berger (Scholastic, 1999): Can it really rain cats and dogs? Who is Jack Frost? Students will become experts when quizzing other children about weather facts. A combination of dramatic pictures and easy-to-read diagrams show young readers the wonder and uncertainty that weather creates on our planet.

I Wonder Why I Blink and Other Questions About My Body by Brigid Airson (Kingfisher, 1993): Teachers will be pleased to present this book as a perfect introduction to the human body. A combination of short paragraphs and matching diagrams help children remember and repeat great facts.

The Reasons for Seasons by Gail Gibbons (Holiday House, 1995): Once again well-known author and illustrator Gail Gibbons takes a complex scientific concept and provides simple and easy diagrams for all ages to enjoy. This book is a must-read for any child during a weather unit.

Surprising Sharks by Nicola Davies (Candlewick Press, 2003): Enter the world of sharks! Children take a dive into the ocean to learn about different types of sharks, what sharks eat, and the major parts of a shark. External and internal shark diagrams are included.

Student Page

Question Cards

Names: ______________________

____

Question: What are three parts of a cat?

Answer: ______________________

____

____

Names: ______________________

____

Question: What are three parts of a tree?

Answer: ______________________

____

____

Names: ______________________

____

Question: How many feet are in a yard?

Answer: ______________________

____

____

Names: ______________________

____

Question: What are the four layers of the rainforest called?

Answer: ______________________

____

____

Question Cards

Names: _____

_____

Question: What are the names of the planets in order from the sun?

Answer: _____

_____

_____

Names: _____

_____

Question: What are the different parts of the water cycle called?

Answer: _____

_____

_____

Names: _____

_____

Question: What oceans surround Australia?

Answer: _____

_____

_____

Names: _____

_____

Question: What are the parts of a bicycle?

Answer: _____

_____

_____

Chapter Four

Captions

Tom was a first grader with a passion for learning about animals. He had a book that was full of beautifully detailed pictures of animals. Tom studied the pictures for hours. He knew that the words under the pictures contained some interesting facts about the animals. He wanted desperately to be able to read those words and learn about the animals. "What does this say?" was Tom's plea to anyone willing and able to read to him. In time, Tom began reading the captions himself.

As readers of nonfiction we know that it is not always necessary to read the entire text. We can use diagrams, photographs, and captions to gather information. Reading captions can be an effective way for the reader to gather information quickly.

Upon reflection, it seems natural that children would have an understanding of captions. Children begin writing stories by drawing pictures and labeling those pictures with words. Eventually, they write sentences explaining their picture. In essence, they are writing captions. It makes sense that they are drawn to the pictures and captions in nonfiction books.

Introduce: What Is a Caption?

A caption is the text that is written to explain a diagram or photograph. It is often located close to the picture. The caption gives the reader information about the picture. Adapt the scripted text that follows to introduce this fun nonfiction feature to students. Use any age-appropriate nonfiction book that contains photographs and captions.

Teacher: *We have been learning about how readers read nonfiction. We've learned that nonfiction text can be read in any order. It does not need to be read from cover to cover like a storybook. We've learned that reading diagrams and labels can give a reader a lot of information. Today we are going to look at the pictures in this book* [read the title] *to see what we can learn about space.* [Take a picture walk through the book, and stop on a page of interest.]

Look at this picture. I wonder what it's a picture of. There are no labels to help me figure out what it is. How can I find out more about this picture? [Guide children to notice the words next to the photo.]

The writing next to the picture is called the caption. Let me show you how readers use captions to get information. I'm wondering about this picture. Now I'm going to read the writing under the picture: "The space probe Mariner 10 is the only one to have visited Mercury so far. In March 1974, Mariner 10 flew less than 440 miles (700 km) above the surface and took thousands of pictures of one side of the planet . . ." [from *Scholastic Atlas of Space* (Scholastic, 2004)] *How did the caption help me as a reader?* [Elicit students' feedback about how captions provide additional information. Then continue looking at other pictures and reading the captions. List information learned from the captions.]

Teaching Tip

Beginning readers and writers are learning that pictures and print convey meaning. Teaching children to read captions in a nonfiction text provides the teacher with opportunities to make important reading-writing connections. Writers write with pictures and words. Readers understand print when they match the words to the pictures.

Explore and Discover

Provide an assortment of nonfiction books with lots of pictures and captions. Then invite students to choose a book to read, and have them record three facts they learn from the captions. Remind students to also record the title and author of the book.

Share and Discuss

Bring students together to share facts they have acquired by reading captions. Invite students to tell what they enjoy about reading captions. Have students reflect on why authors include captions with photographs (or drawings). Ask: *How do captions give readers additional information?* The success in obtaining information by reading a minimal amount of text is empowering to young researchers. As a reminder for students when they read independently, create a chart that highlights important information about reading captions—for example:

❋ A caption is the writing next to a photograph or diagram. It explains the picture.

❋ Writers use captions to include additional information not found in the text.

❋ Readers can look at pictures and read the captions to learn about a topic.

Need More Practice?

To help students understand that a caption describes a diagram or photograph, have them illustrate captions. Give each student a copy of Writing Captions (pages 40–41). Remind children that the picture must match the writing. This exercise will help them see the relationship between the text and picture.

The man was holding a big yellow cat.

The girl in the red dress was standing in front of the yellow house.

Writing Captions

After students have had plenty of opportunity to read captions, give them a chance to write their own. This activity gives children an authentic reason to write, as they create captions for class photos. You'll need photos of students engaged in various activities—these can be everyday activities as well as special events.

1. Explain: *I have an assortment of photos I have taken of our class engaged in a variety of activities at school. I made sure there is a big selection and that every child is pictured in at least one photo.*

2. Choose one of the photos to use in order to model how to write a caption. Say: *Let's take a look at this photo. Can you tell me about it?* Children will be eager to recap the event that is captured in the photo.

3. Invite children to help you write a caption for the photo. Explain: *Before we write the caption, let's think about the purpose of the caption. Remember that the job of the caption is to explain the picture and to give the reader information about it.*

4. Write a caption to go with the photo. Review with students that the caption contains key information, including, as applicable, names, the date, the place, and what's happening.

5. Invite children to each choose a picture and then team up with a partner to share and discuss what's happening in their photo. Encourage students to use this opportunity to fill in any details they may have forgotten and then write their caption.

Children appreciate the very concise nature of captions. Each caption is like a tiny story, conveying key information in a limited amount of space and making attention to word choice very important. Use these ideas to provide practice with writing and reading captions.

Creating a Class Family Album: This lesson correlates with Patricia Polacco's *When Lightning Comes in a Jar* (Penguin, 2002). In this book about a family reunion, the author includes a page from her own family album. A handwritten caption under each photo explains the picture. Let children use the book as inspiration for creating a photo album page of their own (of family, friends, pets, and so on). They can draw pictures or use copies of photographs if available. Have them write captions to describe each picture.

This is my dog Jack. He likes to go for walks.

Create a "How-To" Book: Have children create "how-to" books, complete with pictures and captions. Make sure to choose topics that have only three to four steps. Students can draw diagrams or pictures to show each step and then write corresponding captions. Possible "how-to" topics include:

❋ How to make a peanut butter and jelly sandwich.

❋ How to draw a happy face.

❋ How to build a block tower.

❋ How to wash your hands.

❋ How to get ready for outdoor recess.

❋ How to sign up for lunch.

Write Captions for Artwork: Before displaying students' artwork in the hallway, have them write a caption to hang with their piece.

Use the following selections to provide additional examples of how writers use captions.

Explore and Discover Reptiles by Claire Llewellyn (Kingfisher, 2002): Have you ever wondered what the difference is between an alligator and a crocodile? This book has that answer and more. In addition to using captions to provide additional information on a topic, books in this series have a contents page and an index, a glossary, and a "Look and Find" section.

Eye Wonder: Ocean by Samantha Gray (Dorling Kindersley, 2001): Colorful photos and informative captions take readers on an ocean adventure! Books in this series also include a contents page, sidebars, labels, a glossary, and an index.

I Wonder Why I Blink and Other Questions About My Body by Brigid Avison (Kingfisher, 1993): Why do I get sick? Why do I feel dizzy when I spin around? What is my skin for? These are all questions young learners ask, and this question-and-answer book is a perfect resource for finding the information they're looking for. For connections to other lessons on features of nonfiction, it also features diagrams, labels, and an index.

The Magic School Bus: Inside the Human Body by Joanna Cole (Scholastic, 1989): Every page contains facts written in the captions, speech bubbles, and sidebars. This is also a great book to use when you're comparing fiction and nonfiction text because it contains elements of both. (See page 13.)

Monet by Mike Venezia (Children's Press, 1993): This book is part of the Getting to Know the World's Greatest Artists series, which introduces young readers to well-known artists. Each print is presented with a caption containing the title of the piece and the museum where it is displayed.

One Small Square: Backyard by Donald M. Silver (Freeman, 1991): "With a five-inch wingspan, a black witch moth is as big as a small bird." Information-rich pages in this dazzling book provide many examples of captions filled with fascinating details. Books in the One Small Square series also feature sidebars, diagrams, and an illustrated index.

Scholastic Atlas of Space by Kenneth Wright (Scholastic, 2004): Detailed pages take readers on a tour of the solar system. In addition to captions, this book includes maps, diagrams, an index, and a glossary, making it a rich resource for lessons about nonfiction features.

Shake, Rattle & Roll by Holly George (Houghton Mifflin, 2001): Laura Levine's bold, cartoonlike portraits capture the essence of 14 featured musicians and are accompanied by informative captions.

26 Things Small Hands Do by Coleen Paratore (Free Spirit Publishing, 2004): Highlighted letters on every page will help children review their ABCs while discovering positive actions they can perform with their own small hands. The simple text on each page serves as a caption for the full-page illustration.

Writing Captions

Draw a picture in each box to go with the caption.

Three balloons were floating in the air. One was red, one was blue, and one was green.

The girl in the red dress was standing in front of the yellow house.

Writing Captions

Draw a picture in each box to go with the caption.

The man was holding a
big yellow cat.

Two children were playing
catch in the park.

Chapter Five

Speech Bubbles

A *ren't you going to read the speech bubble?"*
"Can you go back and read what it says in the bubble?"

Until I took the time to sit down with several books that included speech bubbles, I always thought that the bubbles were a waste of time—a break in the information that I really wanted children to understand and learn. It wasn't until I was shopping at a local bookstore that I truly realized the appeal and importance of speech bubbles. As I was looking through the new book display, I stumbled upon a book titled Tall, *by Jez Alborough (Walker Books, 2005). I opened the brightly colored cover to find that the whole book was written in speech bubbles, with very few words in all.* Tall. Small. Tall. Small. *What powerful words for emergent readers to read over and over again. The pictures are beautifully illustrated with a young chimp alternating between feeling small and then tall when he compares himself to other animals. No wonder children are so motivated by speech bubbles. They convey information so concisely, in a fun-to-read format.*

After reading Tall, *I was excited to pack my school bag with several titles that included speech bubbles. Questions immediately came to mind: How do you read the text? Do you read all the bubbles first and then the other text? Or vice versa? Do you read the text in conjunction with the bubbles? These are questions that students ask as well. How do we teach them to read bubbles and get the most information out of these types of texts?*

Introduce: What Is a Speech Bubble?

As children explore nonfiction text, they will notice many variations in the ways in which text appears on the page. There are diagrams, labels, captions, headings, subheadings, and other text features that can make every page look new and different. Speech bubbles are one of the text features they encounter, and students who enjoy comic books will find that they look familiar! A speech bubble is a special feature of text. It usually appears in the shape of a balloon, box, or circle and contains words or thoughts (usually of a character or the narrator) that give readers more information about what's happening on the page. A speech bubble may also have a cloudlike shape. The cloudlike bubbles often contain thoughts rather than dialogue, and are sometimes called thought bubbles. Speech or thought bubbles may or may not contain quotation marks. The scripted lesson that follows is based on *Tall*, but you may also substitute another, such as a book from the Magic School Bus series, that uses speech bubbles to convey information.

Teacher: *Today I am going to share a book with you. This type of book has a different feature that we have not yet discussed but that many of you enjoy and will recognize. When I opened this book, I immediately noticed something different. Do you see this?* [Point to a bubble.] *This is called a speech bubble. How many of you like to look at and read speech bubbles? Why do you think an author would use speech bubbles?* [Brainstorm ideas and list them on chart paper. Reasons might include: to add information that doesn't exactly fit into the text, to show you what someone is saying or thinking, because they are funny, and to "interrupt" the text with a related detail.]

The book I'm going to share with you is Tall, *by Jez Alborough. Listen as I read, and when I am finished, I will ask you to tell me about the speech bubbles.*

When I have finished reading, children quickly raise their hands to share that the story was funny. One child shares that the chimp was his favorite character because on one page the chimp was sad and on the next he was happy. Another child shares that the words *tall*, *small*, and *fall* all rhyme. We continue to explore information that the book shares with readers.

Teacher: *What do you think the word* tall *means? What do you think the word* small *means?*

Child: *My dad is tall. And my cousin is small because she is a baby.*

Child: *A giraffe is tall!*

Teacher: *Boys and girls, when I think of the words* tall *and* small*, they remind me of math. When I am measuring something, I often use the words* tall *and* small *to describe its size. How does this book help you understand the meaning of the words* tall *and* small*?*

Explore and Discover

In advance of the lesson, select nonfiction children's books that feature speech bubbles. (For suggestions, see page 46.) Invite children to choose a book and explore it. Encourage them to refer to the list they created earlier as they think about the author's reason for using speech bubbles. You might also have children use a sticky note to mark a page with a favorite speech bubble.

Share and Discuss

Bring students together to share their discoveries about speech bubbles, including favorite examples. Notice in how many cases the speech bubbles provide information that doesn't quite "fit" with the text on the page. In how many instances do the speech bubbles add humor as well as information? Guide students to notice that speech bubbles often add an element of humor to the page. Students may also notice that the speech bubbles in the books they've been reading are like the speech bubbles they see in comic books and strips.

Need More Practice?

For several days following the initial lesson, model reading different books with speech bubbles. Try a Magic School Bus book, and first read only the bubbles. Then reread the book, this time reading everything but the speech bubbles. Discuss what is useful about reading the book in this order. Another day with a different book, you might read just the regular text and skip the speech bubbles, then return to the beginning and read the speech bubbles. Do students notice new information? Try reading page by page the text then the speech bubbles, and the speech bubbles then the text. Encourage children to try out these and other ways to read books with speech bubbles, and invite them to share strategies they think work best.

Using Speech Bubbles

Children become coauthors of a mini-book that uses speech bubbles to add information that goes beyond the text.

1. Make multiple copies of pages 47–48 (a set for every pair of students). Cut apart the pages, and then place them in order and bind to make each mini-book.

2. Invite students to think about the ways nonfiction authors use speech bubbles to include information that doesn't fit in the text. Revisit a book to remind students that there may be text on a page as well as in a speech bubble. In this case, the speech bubble supports the text with additional information.

3. Give each pair of students a mini-book. Preview the book with students, pointing out that there is text on each page, but the speech bubbles are blank. Explain that students will fill in the speech bubbles with new information to complete the books.

4. Encourage children to use nonfiction books to gather information about their topic (frogs) as they work on adding text to their speech bubbles. Remind them to consider the text already on each page when deciding what to write in the speech bubble.

Teaching Tip

Rather than use the reproducible mini-book provided on pages 47–48, you may choose other topics of interest to your students and use the blank template on page 49 to create your own. Simply copy the template, and then add text, pictures, and a cover to create a master. Then photocopy the mini-book and have students use what they know about the topic to add speech bubble text.

5. When children have completed their books, bring them together to share. Children will be amazed at how different their books are from each other even though the pictures and basic text on each page is the same. They truly see that speech bubbles provide important information.

Teaching Connections and Extensions

Once children learn how to use and read speech bubbles, encourage them to use this text feature in their writing. Challenge them to practice writing speech bubbles for a variety of reasons (refer students to the list they brainstormed).

Rewrite a Wordless Picture Book: *Pancakes for Breakfast*, by Tomie dePaola (Harcourt, 1994), is a great picture story told with no text. Provide speech bubble sticky notes for children to add text to the story. Encourage them to share their versions of the story. Together, notice how many different stories result from the same pictures.

Comic Strip Math: Invite children to solve a math problem comic strip-style. Have them divide a sheet of paper into sections (like a comic strip) and then draw pictures and use speech bubbles to explain their solution to the problem.

Nonfiction Books to Use With This Lesson

These nonfiction titles are fun, informative, and full of speech bubbles!

Look at My Book: How Kids Can Write and Illustrate Terrific Books by Loreen Leedy (Holiday House, 2004): Speech bubbles and supporting text tell readers what they need to know about how authors get ideas, write, and publish.

The Magic School Bus: Inside the Human Body by Joanna Cole (Scholastic, 1989): Fasten your seat belts and prepare for an incredible field trip inside the human body! Factual and fun speech bubbles on every page reinforce and illustrate the reasons for using bubbles.

Millions to Measure by David M. Schwartz (HarperCollins, 2003): Children will love this brightly illustrated book with speech bubbles on almost every page. Fun facts, numbers, and characters' thoughts fill the speech bubbles to show children just how important bubbles can be!

Speech Bubble Mini-Book

Frog at the Pond

By _____

_____

Date _____

1

One day Frog went to the pond.

2

Speech Bubble Mini-Book

Frog was looking for something to eat.

3

Suddenly Frog saw a fly zipping through the air.
Frog jumped and caught the fly just in time!

4

Template for Speech Bubble Mini-Book

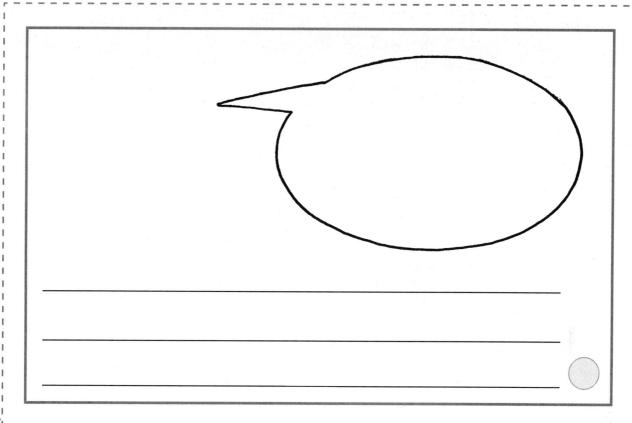

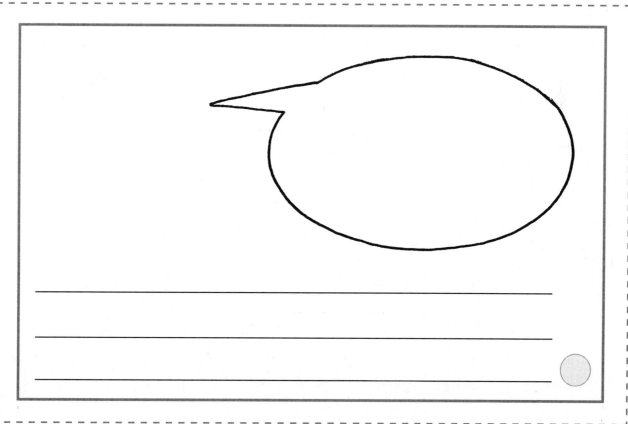

Chapter Six

Maps

I t's late fall and our school is having an open house for families. Excitement is high and children are anxious to "show their stuff."

"I want to show them my story journal," shares Austen.

"They're going to love my research project on tigers," says Samantha.

"I want to be sure they get to see the gym and meet our physical education teacher, Mr. Day," says Connor. "Mr. Day said we could come down to the gymnasium."

Our classmate, Kerstin, who is new to our school this year, is a little worried. "My dad said he is going to come with me, but my mom is going to go with my sister first and then they're going to switch so they can spend some special time with each of us. I don't know how we're going to find each other."

We all agree that it might be helpful for each of us if we make some plans. Together we brainstorm a list of all that there is to see in our classroom and in the school. Our list adds to the excitement, but Kerstin is still concerned.

"I'm still worried that we won't find each other," she says. "My mom and dad don't know very much about this school yet, and we might get lost."

We decide together that it might be helpful for Kerstin to draw a picture of how to get to our classroom and how to get to her sister's classroom. The discussion continues, and it becomes apparent that a "picture" can relay a lot of helpful information.

Mapping is a feature of nonfiction that can take children in many directions. Maps can show information. They can also show direction. Very young learners may visualize a map similar to the way they picture a diagram. Teaching children how to read maps and symbols gives them another tool they can use to better understand what they are reading. Understanding representations of the world requires abstract thinking. However, young children are able to relate due to the pictorial nature of maps.

Introduce: What Is a Map?

A map uses colors, lines, shapes, symbols, and scale to represent places. A legend (key) tells what the symbols mean. A compass rose shows directions on a map. Children will learn that N stands for North, E for East, S for South, and W for West.

Begin an introduction to maps by providing students with access to a class-size set of age-appropriate atlases. After giving students time to browse their atlas, bring them together to share what they notice. Focusing students' attention on the same page to see their classmates' discoveries is a helpful way to negotiate new territory and validate individual learning.

The next step is to introduce students to nonfiction books that contain maps in the context of other information. Take students to the library and have them each find two nonfiction books (not atlases) that contain a map. The books they sign out then become classroom resources.

Upon returning to the classroom, bring students together and have them spread out their books in the middle of the sharing circle. Then it's time to explore the different kinds of maps students found and reasons authors include them. Spend a few minutes first sorting the books into piles by subject—for example, animals, places, and "other."

Teaching Tip

Our students head to the library with "browser bars" in hand. Librarian Kris Larson has students use these tools to mark the location of books they take off the shelves. If they choose not to use a book, they can easily return it to its appropriate spot on the shelf. Wooden paint stirrers make good browser bars. Students can write their names on them to avoid confusion when they take books off the shelf and return them.

Teacher:	[Choose a book and read the title.] New York City, the Big Apple . . . *I can tell from the cover of this book that it probably has maps in it. It's a book about a place, and maps show places. Why do you think an author might use a map in this book?* [for example, to help readers locate special places to see and things to do, to show how big the city is, to show where people live, to show ways to travel to and around the city]
Child:	*It's about New York City! That's where my Grandma lives, so maybe it will show you how to get to her house!*
Teacher:	*You may be right, Joe. It certainly is about New York City.* [Continue with a new book.] *Which book do you think you might use to answer a question about where beavers live?*
Child:	*There are lots of animal books, so it's probably in one of those, but not in this one about farm animals because a beaver is more of a wild animal.*

The discussion continues with similar questions designed to help students locate books by topic and think about the reason for maps in them: *Which book do you think would be helpful in learning where dinosaur bones have been found? Why do you think an author might use a map in this book?* Guide students to notice the legend on a map. Identify what the symbols represent, and discuss how this makes it easier to read a map.

Explore and Discover

Now it's time for students to be map detectives. Invite them to choose a book from the collection and get ready to look more carefully at what the maps tell them. Give each student a copy of the Detective Log (page 57). Review the record sheet with students. Explain that in each section, they will record the subject of a map, the book title and author, the page number, and something they learned by reading the map. Complete one together to be sure students understand what to do:

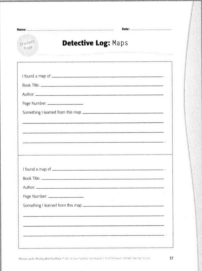

I'll choose this book, Bird's-Eye View, *by Marcia S. Freeman. As I turn the pages I notice that it has lots of maps. The one that interests me most is this one of a river on page nine. On my log I write the name or subject of the map here, "a river map," then the title of the book and the author on the next lines, and the page number on the line that comes after that. The last thing I'm going to do is write something I learned from this map. Something I didn't know that I learned from reading this map is that rivers look like a ribbon because they twist and turn and don't always just go straight.*

Bring students together with their record sheets to share favorite discoveries. From the sample dialogue that follows, you can see that the observations will be quite varied.

Child: *My map showed the place where we live, the United States!*

Child: *My map showed a cool view of a baseball diamond. It was like they took the picture of it from an airplane looking down. I play baseball, but I never thought of it like that before. I wish I could fly on a plane someday!*

Child: *I found a map that looked like a maze only it didn't trick you, it showed you how to get from one place to another.*

Teaching Tip

Based on your students' needs and abilities, you may choose to have them complete a log for one map before bringing them together to share or give them time to complete the log for up to four maps.

Students will no doubt be experiencing a growing confidence with their new map finding and reading skills. Many will be anxious to go back and read more about the places and information they found mapped in their books. Help children synthesize what they've learned by creating and displaying a poster about maps. You might include on the poster an actual map with labels that identify different parts of the map (compass rose, key or legend, title), and explain how they help readers.

What We Know About Maps

❉ There are many kinds of maps.

❉ Some maps show cities, states, countries, or the world.

❉ Some maps show where animals live.

❉ Some maps show where mountains or oceans or lakes are.

❉ Maps can show direction or represent information.

❉ A key explains the symbols on a map.

❉ A compass rose shows North, South, East, and West. The abbreviations are N, S, E, and W.

❉ Some books are full of just maps (atlases).

❉ Some books include a map to represent a lot of information in a small space.

❉ Maps usually have a title or a caption that explains them.

The study of maps lends itself nicely to computer work. Have students bring their detective logs to a computer lab, if available, and further research a topic to find different maps. Students can easily learn to type in a key word in a search engine to find lots of maps related to a topic. For example, students might go to google.com and type in "Amazon Rainforest Maps."

Making Maps

Kerstin's problem (page 50) was just one example of the ways in which children are quick to point out reasons to make maps in their own lives. Practice in making maps of familiar places will personalize each student's learning. Making a map for authentic use, as in Kerstin's case, is an even more powerful opportunity for practice. The classroom, playground, school, home, and neighborhood are certainly places with which students are familiar enough to make their own maps. Use the directions that follow to make a map of your town. With a shower curtain as its base, this map folds up to store away easily and withstands lots of use . . . which is helpful, because "driving around town" soon becomes a favorite choice-time activity!

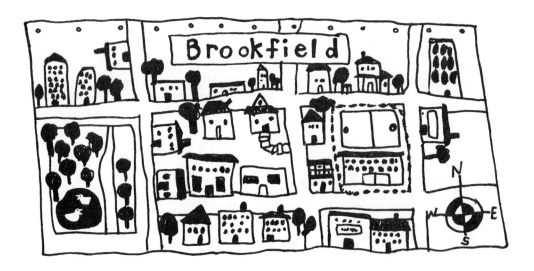

1. Share a book of detailed maps that show how to get somewhere. *National Geographic Big Book of Maps* (National Geographic Society, 2001) is a good choice.

2. Look closely at several maps with students and notice roads, signs, buildings, trees, houses, and other landmarks.

3. Explain that students are going to work together to make a map of their community. Ask: *What kinds of buildings and special landmarks will we need to include to be sure it shows our town?*

4. Together, brainstorm a list—for example, shops, the fire station, different schools, students' homes, a park, and the police station.

5. Place a shower curtain (or large sheet of paper) on the floor and explain that this will be the map. Work with students to plot out a representation of the town, using permanent marker to draw main roads.

6. Give children precut white drawing paper (sized for the map) and invite them to draw various items to include on their map (homes, parks, shops, the library, and so on). (Make a list with students in advance of special landmarks they can sign up to draw.)

7. Affix the drawings to the map with clear contact paper. Use permanent marker to add signs, trees, or other details as desired. Complete the map with a title and a compass rose showing north, south, east, and west.

Teaching Connections and Extensions

As children get to know themselves as readers, they become increasingly skilled at choosing books that are "just right." To help them develop strategies around applying those skills to books with maps, try this activity.

Choosing "Just Right" Maps: Display a collection of atlases that range from primary to upper elementary, middle school, high school, and even college level. Choose selections that will allow children to compare a geographic area they are familiar with, such as their state or the United States, to really illustrate the difference in detail. Invite them to compare the way the map of this area looks in each book. Children easily note that these books are just like the fiction books with which they are familiar: Print size, number of "pictures" (in this case, maps), and length of the book are all indicators of how difficult it will be for the reader to understand. Even though maps are "pictures," establish that some are easier to "read" than others.

Teaching Tip

We use the "Goldilocks Rule" when deciding what book is "just right" for us as readers. A book should not be too hard or too easy . . . it should be just right! Students can learn to preview books for different criteria, such as text size, number of pictures, number of words, and text features to decide how to make appropriate choices of readability.

Our Map Discoveries:
Keep a class chart of the different styles or types of maps students discover in their reading—for example, physical, political, weather, population, and attractions. (See sample, right.)

Our Map Discoveries		
Kind of Map	**Where We Found It**	**Page #**
Physical map of Vermont	Junior Atlas	24
Political map of the U.S.A.	Primary Atlas	6
Where animals live	National Geographic Big Book of Maps	2
Special places to see	National Geographic Big Book of Maps	4

Nonfiction Books to Use With This Lesson

From a bird's-eye view of a baseball field to an atlas of an ocean, the maps in these books will motivate students to continue exploring representations of the world around them.

A Bird's-Eye View by Marcia S. Freeman (Rand McNally, 1999): Dramatic illustrations provide a unique perspective of places in every child's world—the neighborhood, a baseball diamond, and many more.

Discovering El Niño by Patricia Seibert (Millbrook Press, 1999): Selected as an Outstanding Science Trade Book for Children, this picture book is full of colorful illustrations and interesting text. Maps support the text and clarify the scientific information.

Junior Classroom Atlas (Rand McNally, 2001): This appealing collection includes political, physical, climate, and land use maps. Adjoining pictures with captions extend the information readers are able to gather.

Map Keys by Rebecca Aberg (Scholastic, 2003): This superb instructional book for young researchers contains simple, straightforward, and informative text and graphics.

National Geographic Big Book of Maps (National Geographic Society, 2001): The beautifully detailed maps in this varied collection are large enough to share with a whole class. This book includes a beginning section on simple neighborhood maps and continues with colorful maps of places around the world.

Primary Atlas (Rand McNally, 2002): This colorful collection of simple, political maps of the United States and the continents of the world includes engaging sidebar photographs of landmarks.

Scholastic Atlas of Oceans by Donna Vekteris (Scholastic, 2004): Detailed and engaging maps ensure that every young reader will learn a new exciting fact about the ocean. This resource offers many opportunities to explore cross-referencing information among the contents page, glossary, index, and maps.

Types of Maps by Mary Dodson Wade (Scholastic, 2003): Simple yet meaningful examples of maps combine with clear explanations to make this a good resource for young readers.

Detective Log: Maps

- -

I found a map of _____ .

Book Title: _____

Author: _____

Page Number: _____

Something I learned from this map _____

_____

_____

_____ .

I found a map of _____ .

Book Title: _____

Author: _____

Page Number: _____

Something I learned from this map _____

_____

_____

_____ .

Chapter Seven

Glossaries

Mrs. Farnham, Mrs. Farnham! I just heard that word we learned about yesterday!"

We had just begun our day and already Amy was full of excitement. "What word is that?" I asked.

"You know, that word literacy. We just learned it yesterday. Remember, reading, writing, speaking, and listening?"

"Nice listening," I confirmed. "When did you hear it?"

"Just now! We all said it in the Pledge of Allegiance. You know, at the end we say, "and literacy, just for us all!"

What a warm feeling this true story brings to my heart. We send our charges out into the world as detectives looking to practice their newfound knowledge, and they take their work so seriously.

Introduce: What Is a Glossary?

Readers can find the glossary at the back of a book. A glossary lists important words from the text in alphabetical order. It tells what the words mean and may include a pronunciation key. When words in the text appear in boldfaced type, this is usually a sign to readers that those words are defined in a glossary. Introduce students to this feature of nonfiction by sharing an example of how a glossary helps you prepare for a lesson. This lesson is based on a specific book (*Animal Homes*, by Tammy Everts and Bobbie Kalman; Crabtree, 1994), but you can easily substitute another text with a glossary.

Teacher: *I was getting ready last night for our work today in science by reading the book* Animal Homes, *by Tammy Everts and Bobbie Kalman. I noticed that some of the words were darker than other words on the page. This is called boldfaced print. Here are some of the words that I found in boldface:* instinct, sentry, chamber, warren, bolthole, *and* termitaries. *I thought, "These must be important words since they're written in this special way." They're difficult words, too, and I wasn't sure of the meaning of all of them. For example, I know* warren *can be a man's name, but in that case it would have an uppercase* W. *So I know the book isn't talking about a man. I wondered: "What can I do to find out what the word* warren *means in this book?"*

Children quickly come up with the dictionary as a resource for finding meanings of words.

Teacher: *You're exactly right! But there's a special feature right here in this book called a glossary that can help readers understand these words. A glossary is a page or two in the book that lists important or difficult words and their definitions and often tells you how to pronounce them. It's a lot like a dictionary but much shorter. Sometimes a glossary may have a different title, such as "Special Words" or "Words to Know." Also, not all books have a glossary. So now I will look at this book's glossary to find out what the word* warren *means. I know that the list is in alphabetical order, and* warren *starts with a letter that is near the end of the alphabet. So I can zoom right to the end of the list. Here it is: A warren is a rabbit's home! Now when I go back to the chapter where I found this word, I will have a great picture in my head of what this word means.*

Explore and Discover

Invite children to work with partners as they look through the class collection of nonfiction books to locate glossaries. Have them read the words they find together and discuss their meanings. Before children get started, remind them that the glossary is often, but not always, in the back of the book near the index. Encourage them to notice if they find lists of words that have a different title than "glossary." To take their explorations further, give children copies of New Word Finders (page 63) to keep track of favorite words in glossaries and their meanings.

Need More Practice?

To reinforce the process of using a glossary, give students time to both read and write about the information they find. Make available copies of New Word Finders. As your students read independently and find new words in glossaries, have them record a few select words. Remind them to read through the list of words in the glossary first and choose words of particular interest to them that they did not know before.

Share and Discuss

Bring students together to share glossaries they located, words they found especially interesting, and then give the meanings as well. Encouraging this interest in discovering new words is a great way to build vocabulary and help children develop a thirst to learn more. List students' words on chart paper for later use. (See Reading-Writing Connections: Wonderful Words Glossary, page 61.) After sharing their words, involve children in creating a poster that lists helpful things to remember about glossaries.

What We Know About Glossaries

❋ like a mini-dictionary

❋ lists challenging words and tells their meaning

❋ often in the back of the book

❋ not all nonfiction books have a glossary

❋ may be called Words to Know or something else

❋ words are listed in ABC order

❋ sometimes shows how to say the word (pronunciation)

❋ words in a glossary may be in boldfaced type (or italics) in the text

As children continue to read nonfiction on their own, encourage them to keep in mind that even though the glossary might be at the back of the book, it's a good idea to locate the glossary before you start reading, and to take a look at the words in it. This will give them an idea of what words are important in the text, and they'll know where to look if they need to know more about these words as they read.

Reading-Writing Connections

Wonderful Words Glossary

A class wall glossary is a helpful tool all year as students "read around the room" to refresh their skills. It also serves as a springboard for communication when parents or other guests come to visit.

1. Write each of the words students shared (See Share and Discuss, page 60) on an index card. Place the cards in a basket.

2. Give each student one card to begin. Explain that you want students to look up their word in a dictionary and write the definition in their own words on the card (next to the word). Remind students to use their best handwriting because they will display their words and definitions on the wall so that everyone can learn from them. (You might also provide opportunities to use a computer to type and print the definition, and then glue that on the card.)

3. When students finish one card, they can help themselves to another.

4. Label a space on the wall "Wonderful Words Glossary." Decide with students whether the words will be organized on the wall in general ABC order or possibly in ABC order by topic or subject area. Add to the words as students come across new content-specific vocabulary in their reading that they want to share. (Using sticky tack to place the cards on the wall will make it easier to insert new words in alphabetical order.)

Teaching Tip

Gooney Bird and the Room Mother, by Lois Lowry (Houghton Mifflin, 2005), is a wonderful read aloud that supports through its story line the discovery of new and interesting words (and investigation of their meaning). Gooney Bird loves to share challenging words with her second-grade classmates, and *incognito* becomes one of them as she sets out to find her teacher a desperately needed room mother in time for the Thanksgiving pageant. She succeeds in her search, but only with the condition that the person remain *incognito* until the big day arrives.

Use these suggestions to create a general curiosity and awareness for identifying challenging words in daily work.

Class Chart of Challenging Words: Keep an ongoing class chart of difficult words. (See sample, right.) Students can add to it as they come across challenging vocabulary in any of their reading. Consider using some of students' newly found words as spelling challenges! You may also add the words to your Word Wall.

Big Words Bookmarks: Words as small as *pig* and as long as *alligator* can all be "big" words to young readers. Make bookmarks children can use to record words that they find especially challenging or interesting as they read. Simply cut card stock into bookmarks, have children write their names on one, and let the word gathering begin! Every now and then, take time to let students share words they've added to their bookmarks. Encourage them to let you know when they decide one of these words is just right to use in a piece of their own writing.

New Words

ennui
indefatigable
incognito
cajole
fiasco
admonition

This sample chart features words from the class favorite *Gooney Bird and the Room Mother* (see Teaching Tip, page 61).

Nonfiction Books to Use With This Lesson

From *tide* to *praying mantis*, the words in these books will have children exploring glossaries and acquiring all sorts of new vocabulary.

Animal Homes by Tammy Everts and Bobbie Kalman (Crabtree, 1994): Playful and colorful illustrations totally engage the reader. Boldfaced vocabulary signals the reader to use the glossary to find out even more about the fascinating information on each page.

The Best Book of Bugs by Claire Llewellyn (Kingfisher, 1998): Brightly illustrated pages with artwork that articulately represents a variety of insects combine with rich, scientific vocabulary to help little readers become big scientists.

Scholastic Atlas of Oceans by Donna Vekteris (Scholastic, 2004): Each page encourages children to explore facts, activities, and trivia about the amazing ocean and its creatures. Teachers will have a hard time choosing among all the important nonfiction features to highlight in this text (including a glossary)!

Usborne Internet-Linked First Encyclopedia of the Human Body by Fiona Chandler (Usborne, 2004): Look inside to find an abundance of information organized in a very accessible way for young researchers as they begin to appreciate the use of an encyclopedia as a resource.

Name: _____ **Date:** _____

Student Page

New Word Finders

Choose a nonfiction book to read.

Make sure it has a glossary. Then fill in the blanks.

New Word Finders

Book Title: _____

Author: _____

New Word: _____

Definition: _____

New Word Finders

Book Title: _____

Author: _____

New Word: _____

Definition: _____

Chapter Eight

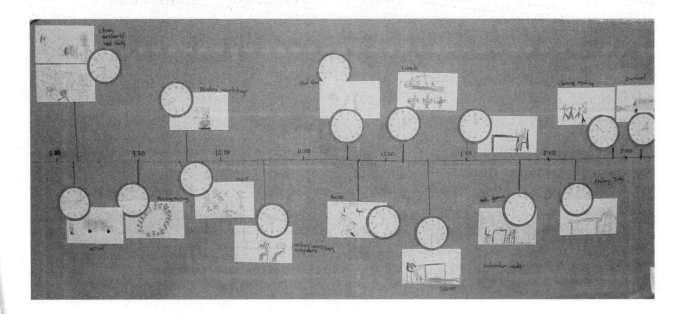

Time Lines

H"ow old are you?" asked one of my first graders.

"How old do you think I am?" I reply, curious to hear his answer.

"Twenty-five?" he says.

"Why, thank you!" I am delighted with his idea that I am nearly half my age.

He smiles. "Was I right?"

To him, 25 years seems like an awfully long time. Time is such an abstract concept for young children to grasp. Yet they seem to be consumed with wonder about it and its relation to them. Susie proudly states, "I'm older than Tom because my birthday is before his!"

Capitalizing on this fascination with age, I introduce my students to time lines early in the year by creating a birthday time line. On individual sheets of paper, I write each child's name and birth date (month, date, and year). Children decorate their paper in some way *(a picture of a birthday wish, a favorite birthday, a self-portrait). Together we lay the papers out on the floor chronologically, starting with the child who was born first. This time line hangs on our wall throughout the rest of the year and is our first experience with this graphic aid.*

Although our birthday time line spans only two years, it serves as an illustration of a sequence of events happening over time. Providing children with concrete representations of abstract concepts in this way helps them to better understand the concept. They can then use their knowledge of time lines they create, such as for birth dates, to understand time lines in books they read.

Introduce: What Is a Time Line?

A time line is a special type of diagram. It shows a series of events and the dates on which the events happened. Time lines show events in a visually simple way. They enable the reader to visualize and better understand a series of events. Time lines allow the reader to obtain information and see the relationship between and among events within a time period at a glance. Events spanning a large amount of time can be shown on one page. We use a favorite fiction selection, *Ox-Cart Man*, by Donald Hall (Viking, 1979), to introduce a lesson on time lines. Students can easily tell from the events and illustrations that the story took place many years ago. This presents an opportunity to use a time line to show that time span relative to events in their own lives.

Teaching Tip

You may often find that a fictional story works well to teach or introduce a nonfiction feature. In particular, historical fiction (such as *Ox-Cart Man*, used in this lesson) lends itself to a study of time lines.

Teacher: *Today we are going to read a story called* Ox-Cart Man, *by Donald Hall. As you listen, see if you can tell when it took place.* [After reading the book, we discuss things that happened in the story that let the reader know that this story took place many years ago.]

We can tell from the way the ox-cart man and his family lived that they lived a long time ago. They lived in the 1830s. That was 177 years ago! [To demonstrate how long ago 1830 was, I use a tape measure. I pull out the tape 177 inches. Zero represents today (2007) and 177 inches represents 1830 (177 years ago). I lay the tape measure on the floor. Next to zero I place an index card that reads "2007: Today" and a card next to 177 that says "1830: The Ox-Cart Man." We then add some events from children's lives.]

Teacher: *How old are you?*

Child: *I'm 8.*

Teacher: *Let's find 8 on the tape measure. This is how many years ago you were born. Do you know what year you were born?*

Child: *1999.* [I write "1999: Ann was born" on an index card and place it next to the numeral 8, because Ann is 8 years old.]

Teacher: *I was born in 1956. That was 51 years ago. Who can point to 50 on the tape measure?* [On a card I write "1956: Mrs. Kulhowvick was born" and place it next to 51. We continue with a few other historic events (such as the building of our school, founding of our town, first airplane flight, and invention of the television), and place them on our time line.]

Teacher: *We have created a time line. A time line is a special kind of diagram that shows events happening over time.*

Child: *Like our birthday time line!* [They immediately make the connection to our birthday time line.]

Teacher: *That's right! Our birthday time line shows the dates you were born. Authors sometimes use time lines to help the reader understand when events happened. Let's look at one together. Then you'll have time to explore them on your own.*

Together, look at a time line in an age-appropriate nonfiction book. Point out the title, and invite students to identify key words that tell them what the time line is about. Identify the starting and ending dates. Is this time line showing current events or events in history? Notice if the time line is horizontal or vertical. (Try to show examples of each.) Explain how this helps you know in which direction to read the time line (left to right or top to bottom). Read the labels for at least some of the dates. Point out how they relate to the title.

Explore and Discover

On students' work tables, display several books with time lines. Let children know they will share the books with others at their table. Have them find the time lines in the books and look at them together. Explain that you want them to think about what they notice about the time lines: Does the time line have a title? What is the starting and ending date? What does the time line show? If they were going to tell a classmate about the information on this time line, what would they say?

Bring students together to discuss similarities and differences among the time lines. Record their comments about time lines on a chart. Guide them to discover characteristics that time lines have in common: They have a title; they all tell the time that each event happened, and they tell about each event in words and/or pictures. Time lines often have an introduction that tells about the information included. Students also discover that time lines are easy to read and understand. Discuss why authors may choose to include time lines in their nonfiction books and how they can help readers better understand the text. Display what students know about time lines on a poster to provide helpful reminders when they read independently.

What We Know About Time Lines

❋ **Title:** Tells you the topic of the time line.

❋ **Introduction:** Tells you what kind of information you will find in the time line.

❋ **Dates:** Shows how much time is covered in the time line. The dates in between are in order and tell you the date that each event took place.

❋ **Labels and Captions:** Give you more information about each event.

Over the next several days, look at various time lines with children. Choose time lines with different formats—for example, horizontal and vertical, with text boxes or picture boxes, and with and without an introduction. Encourage students to pay close attention to the parts of the time line (title, introduction, times/dates, labels, and captions), and discuss with them how to read each time line. This continued practice with time lines will help children develop the skills they need with the various parts of a time line so that they can easily access information from them.

As you examine each time line with children, ask questions to guide their understanding:

❋ What is this time line about?

❋ Where can we look to find out?

❋ What kind of information can we get from the time line?

❋ What do you now know about [topic] from reading the time line?

❋ Why do you think [author] put time lines in this book? How did this time line help you better understand [topic]?

Individual Time Lines

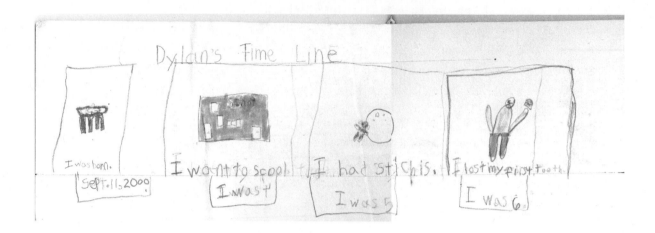

After exploring time lines in books, let students apply what they've learned by creating their own. A time line of important events in their lives builds in a level of familiarity, so children can more easily focus on the parts of their time line (title, introduction, times/dates, labels, and captions).

1. Model the activity for children by creating a time line of important events in your life for some period of time. Think aloud about how you decide whether your time line will be vertical or horizontal. What is the starting date? Ending? Fill in events, using words and graphics to provide important information. Point out how the dates are in order from top (earliest) to bottom (most recent). Explain how this helps readers make sense of the information. Think aloud about a title for your time line, and then write a brief introduction.

2. Let students read and discuss your time line to reinforce their understanding of each part. Ask: *What do you know about me from reading my time line? How do each of these parts I've included—title, introduction, and so on—help you read and understand my time line?*

Teaching Tip

In a note home, you may want to ask families to help out by sending in a list of significant events in their children's lives. For children who are unable to bring this information from home, you might conference about events that have been important in school, such as the day a child read his or her first book or lost a tooth.

3. Give each child a copy of the time line template (page 71). Guide children in cutting apart the two strips and gluing them together at the tabs. Then have them glue their time line to a larger sheet of paper. Review that this is a horizontal time line. Ask: *Do you remember how to read this kind of time line?* (from left to right) *On what date will your time line begin?*

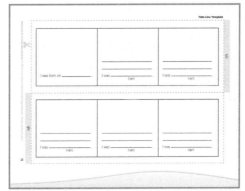

4. To complete the time line, have children first draw a picture to represent the day they were born, and then complete the sentence by filling in their birth date. For each additional box, have children draw a picture representing an important event, and then write a sentence about it and fill in their age. Finally, have them give their time line a title and write an introduction.

Teaching Connections and Extensions

Look to content area topics of study for opportunities to strengthen students' ability to make sense of the way time lines organize information.

Biography Time Lines: As part of a unit on biographies, have students read a biography about a person in history and create a time line about that person's life.

Life Cycle Time Lines: Any science unit on life cycles such as plants or insects would be perfect for creating time lines to show the growth and changes that take place over the life span. If you are learning about seasonal changes, you could make a time line of a tree throughout the year.

Math Time Lines: Use time lines as part of a math unit on telling time. Children can create individual time lines about their own day from the time they get up to the time they go to bed. They can include graphics of clocks to depict the times shown.

Time Line Story Retelling: As a literacy connection, use time lines to retell a story. Children will have fun creating a time line to retell familiar stories such as *The Three Bears. Nantucket Cats,* by Dawn Watkins (BJU Press, 1998), is a delightful story of a group of clever cats and their excursion on Nantucket Island. This is not only an excellent book to help teach children how to tell time but a great one to retell through a time line. Eric Carle's *The Grouchy Ladybug* (HarperCollins, 1996) is another excellent example of a story that spans time. It would be a wonderful story to retell as a time line.

Calendar Sequence: For young learners, cut apart an old calendar and have them sequence the months in correct order. Write a day of the week on each of seven index cards and ask children to sequence them in order.

Nonfiction Books to Use With This Lesson

Try these titles to provide practice with reading time lines.

Emergency! by Gail Gibbons (Scholastic, 1994): Gibbons provides the reader with three very simple time lines of emergency vehicles throughout history. Children will be able to see at a glance police cars, ambulances, and fire trucks of the past. These are nice examples to use to begin introducing time lines to children.

Let Freedom Ring: Benedict Arnold by Susan R. Gregson (Bridgestone Books, 2002): This book is part of a series that explores topics and events from important periods in America's past. Nonfiction features included in these books are contents, time lines (including excellent examples of a linear time line), maps, diagrams, captions, sidebars, glossary, and index.

The Magic School Bus: In the Time of the Dinosaurs by Joanna Cole (Scholastic, 1994): Cole incorporates several time lines in this book, each one simply drawn and easy to understand. They are perfect examples when introducing time lines.

A Picture Book of . . . Series by David A. Adler (Scholastic, 1998): Several different books in this series feature a list of important events and dates in the lives of historical figures including Amelia Earhart, George Washington, Harriet Tubman, and Jesse Owens.

Time for Kids Biographies (HarperCollins, 2006): This series provides young readers with a close-up look at important people in history. It features historical and contemporary photographs as well as interviews with experts. A time line of key dates in the person's life is located at the end of the book.

We the People: The Underground Railroad by Ann Heinrichs (Compass Point Books, 2001): This book is part of a series about key events in U.S. history, and features a glossary, lists of important dates and people, a Did You Know? and Want to Know More? section, and an index. Important dates are written in the form of a time line.

Who Was Johnny Appleseed? by Joan Holub (Grosset & Dunlap, 2005): This book is one in a series of biographies of historical figures. Each book features a time line of the person's life along with a time line of the world, which encourages comparisons and connections.

tab

I was _____
_____
_____ (age)

I was _____
_____
_____ (age)

I was _____
_____ (age)

I was born on _____
_____

I was _____
_____
_____ (age)

I was _____
_____
_____ (age)

tab

Chapter Nine

Comparisons

It is September 17, my birthday! The teacher's birthday is always a very exciting day in an elementary school. It doesn't take long for children to ask the inevitable question, "How old are you?"

I respond with, "Well, let me ask you a question: Who do you think is older, Mr. O'Brien or me?"

"Mr. O'Brien!" they declare.

This leads to a discussion that naturally involves comparisons. When asked why they think Mr. O' Brien is older, children explain that it's because "Mr. O' Brien has been married a long time," "Mr. O' Brien has kids and you do not," and "Mr. O' Brien wears glasses." Without knowing it, children are making comparisons between me and our principal. They are identifying physical characteristics that separate the two of us and make us different.

Isn't it true that children make comparisons all day long? They are always very quick to notice that the older children have PE for a longer period of time and that someone in our snack circle got six crackers and another person got only four. As I reflect on the comparisons that children naturally make in the course of an ordinary day, I realize all the important math and science information that I can teach them by specifically pointing out comparisons in text and teaching them how to make connections and visualize what these comparisons mean.

Introduce: What Is a Comparison?

To compare is to note the similarities and differences between two things. Authors use this text structure as a way of organizing information. Comparing and contrasting two subjects helps readers understand what is the same and what is different. Introduce this text structure to students, using a familiar math manipulative: Unifix cubes. In advance of the lesson, prepare a long chain of 50 linked Unifix cubes. Alternate two colors in groups of ten each—for example, ten red, ten yellow, ten red, ten yellow, ten red (so the chain begins and ends with the same color).

Teacher: *Last night I went home and built something special for our math class. Let's look at what I made. You recognize these cubes from math, but we can also use them to learn something new about nonfiction books we read. What do you notice about my new tool?*

Child: *I notice that it looks like you used a lot of cubes.*

Child: *I noticed that you used two different colors.*

Teacher: *You are right. I did use a lot of cubes and in two different colors. How many do you think I used?*

Child: *61.*

Child: *1,000!*

Child: *I know that there are ten red and then ten yellow. That means that we could count by tens to figure out the answer.*

Teacher: *Good noticing! Can you all count by tens with me to help find out how many cubes I used?*

Children: *10, 20, 30 . . . 50!*

Teacher: *Boys and girls, I want you to look around our room and see if you can find anything that looks as if it would be shorter than 50 cubes.* [Children respond with objects such as a pencil, a book, and a ruler, which I record on a T-chart.]

Comparisons

Longer	Shorter
door	pencil
table	book
rug	ruler

Teacher: *Now look around the room and search for items that look longer than 50 cubes.* [Children are eager to respond with items such as the height of the door, the length of a table, and the distance around our area rug.]

Nice thinking! You were all just comparing different objects to one tool, my 50 cubes. I want to show you a page in one of my favorite books about measuring. This book is called Millions to Measure, *by David Schwartz* [HarperCollins, 2003]. *It is a book all about how we measure different objects in our country. Today I am not going to read the whole book to you. I am going to flip to page 12. What do you notice about this page?*

Child: *I can tell by the diagram that the snake is longer than the pencil. The pencil is about three inches long and the snake is about 12 inches long.*

Teacher: *This diagram is an example of a comparison. The author compared two different objects using the same tool. You already practiced that skill today when you looked around the room for objects that were longer and shorter than my 50 cubes. Now let's see if the author also makes comparisons in the text.*

Read aloud a portion of the text in which the author describes two things to highlight similarities and differences—for example, in *Millions to Measure*, the author compares a snake to a ruler. Invite children to identify what was compared and what they learned. Point out key words in the text, such as *inch, foot,* and *length,* that signal a comparison. Other examples of signal words found in this text structure are *like, unlike, but, in contrast, on the other hand, however, both, also, too,* and *as well as.* Then send children off to explore and discover, looking for more examples of comparisons in nonfiction books. (See below.)

Explore and Discover

Have children work independently or with partners to preview and read nonfiction books, looking for examples of comparisons. Review that there are different ways authors might compare and contrast. For example, they might make comparisons in the text or organize the information in diagrams that compare one thing to another. When students find an example, have them mark it with a sticky note. Remind students that when it's time to share and discuss their discoveries, the sticky notes will help them quickly find their examples. (Students can move their sticky notes into their journals or learning logs and add more detail, including labels and captions that help explain their comparisons.)

As children work, meet with small groups to point out different types of comparisons in their books, such as two pints compared to one quart and the size of an elephant compared to an adult human. Guide children to notice key words the authors of their books use to make comparisons. You might also suggest particular examples for children to mark to ensure that when you bring the class together for a discussion, you have the examples you want to highlight.

Teaching Tip

Ahead of time, stock several baskets with nonfiction books in different categories, such as science and math. This will help ensure the success of all students. I also offer *Millions to Measure* to a student who may have trouble getting started. This book will be sure to jump-start any reader, especially since it is recommended by the teacher!

Bring children together to share their examples of comparisons. Encourage them to explain why they think the author decided to make a comparison. For example, an author writing about an animal might compare its size to that of a human to help readers visualize just how big (or small) the animal is. Discuss with children the importance of noticing comparisons in nonfiction text they read. Point out that by making comparisons, or showing likenesses and differences, authors give readers information to help them better understand the topic.

Need More Practice?

Continue to provide students with opportunities to make concrete comparisons—for example, use colorful electrical tape to create a large Venn diagram on the floor. Use it to compare children's favorites (such as books, fruits, and colors). For example, label one circle "Apples" and another "Bananas." Let children sort themselves by the fruit they prefer, with those who like both arranging themselves in the intersecting area of the circles. Invite children to make comparisons based on the Venn diagram. Encourage them to use signal words in their statements—for example, "Coby and Mia both like apples. Lauren does, too. But Howie prefers bananas." Along with these comparisons, continue to model how you notice and make sense of comparisons in different books you read with students.

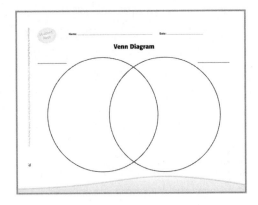

Provide copies of the Venn diagram on page 79 for students to make additional comparisons.

Reading-Writing Connections

Class Book of Comparisons

Introduce this writing activity by sharing a book that invites comparisons: *Actual Size*, by Steve Jenkins (Houghton Mifflin, 2004). This book contains information about animals from around that world that are unusually big and small, with striking collage illustrations that let readers grasp just how big or small that is. (For more information on this title, see Nonfiction Books to Use With This Lesson, page 78.)

1. Share the book's cover and invite children to describe what they see. (There is a picture of a hand on the cover. A tiny pygmy mouse lemur is sitting on the thumb.) Remind children of times they have used their hands to make measurements. Ask how the size of the animal on the cover compares to that of the hand.

2. Share the book with students and let them take turns on different pages comparing the size of their hand with the size of the animal pictures.

3. Take further the idea of using their hand as a way to measure and make comparisons. Have children think of something in the classroom they could compare to the size of their hand in order to give someone a good sense of just how big or small the object is. (Examples of responses are "How about a tack? A tack is really small!" and "The clock is a lot bigger than my hand.")

4. Create a class book that will remind students of what the word *comparison* means. Have each student choose one object to compare to his or her hand. Tell students to trace the shape of the object on a sheet of paper to make sure that the

picture is actual size. Remind students that some of the animals in *Actual Size* did not fit completely on the pages in the book. Explain that, in the same way, some of their objects will be bigger than the size of their paper. Have students recall what the author did when the animal was too big to show in its entirety on the page. (The author then pictured part of the animal in actual size.)

5. Select an object, such as a clock, that you can't picture in actual size in its entirety. Model how to trace part of the clock on the paper and color it as it appears (including only those numbers that appear in the section that fits). Label the important parts of the drawing and give it a title. Use your hand to measure the object and make a comparison—for example, "My clock hand is longer than my hand."

6. Let students find their own objects to picture actual size and then label their drawing and give it a title.

7. Collect students' completed drawings to make a class book. Add a front and back cover and bind.

Teaching Connections and Extensions

From attendance graphs to water table investigations, everyday classroom activities invite comparisons.

Daily Attendance: Use the information displayed on the daily attendance chart or graph to make comparisons—for example, "Are there more students here today than there were yesterday? Three children were absent yesterday, and there are three missing today, too."

Morning Meeting Measurements: Use this meeting time to generate discussion about similarities and differences children see in books, the weather, and so on. Encourage them to identify measuring tools (such as years, inches, hands) they can use to make comparisons. For example, looking at a weekly weather graph, children might notice, "We used a thermometer to measure the temperature in degrees. Monday was cold, but Wednesday was even colder!"

Water Table Discoveries: During a study of comparisons, make the water table available during explore time. Include different measuring devices to encourage children to compare the amounts of liquid that fit in each container.

Great Glyphs: During science time, have children complete glyphs that relate to what they are studying. A glyph is a picture representation that is colored or decorated according to characteristics. For example, make glyphs to go with a study of the weather. Give each student a picture of an umbrella. Have children who prefer rainy days color the handle black. Have children who prefer sunny days color the handle yellow. Have children who like both kinds of weather color the handle green. To continue, invite children to color the top of the umbrella according to the temperature they prefer. If they like hot weather, have them color it red. If they like cooler temperatures, have them color it blue. If they like both hot and cold weather, have them color it red with blue dots. Have children sort their glyphs in different ways according to that data.

Nonfiction Books to Use With This Lesson

Try these titles to provide practice with identifying comparisons as a text structure.

Actual Size by Steve Jenkins (Houghton Mifflin, 2004): Striking collage illustrations bring animals to life in this fact-filled book. Each animal or part of an animal is shown in actual size—from the entire 36-inch Gippsland earthworm to the eye of a giant squid. Using the cover illustration as inspiration (a tiny creature perched on the thumb of a hand), children will love placing their tiny hand on each page to make comparisons.

Fannie in the Kitchen by Deborah Hopkinson (Simon & Schuster, 2001): Cooking is a great way to encourage children to practice comparisons. Which is more, $2/3$ or $3/4$ cup of flour? This wonderful story of cooking also has a great recipe for griddle cakes at the end!

Hottest, Coldest, Highest, Deepest by Steve Jenkins (Houghton Mifflin, 1998): This Caldecott Honor winner leads you through a journey of different countries' terrain to investigate the longest river, deepest lake, and coldest place. The text is filled with mathematical language and visual representations that illustrate simple comparisons.

Millions to Measure by David M. Schwartz (HarperCollins, 2003): This Horn Honor Book for illustration draws children in with rich colors and animated illustrations while teaching about the history of measurement. Pictorial representations and comparisons help students grasp conversions and other measuring concepts.

Surprising Sharks by Nicole Davies (Candlewick Press, 2003): If you are studying oceans, this is a must-read. Open to page one to find a comparison of 12 different sharks, including their sizes and physical characteristics.

Name: _____

Date: _____

Venn Diagram

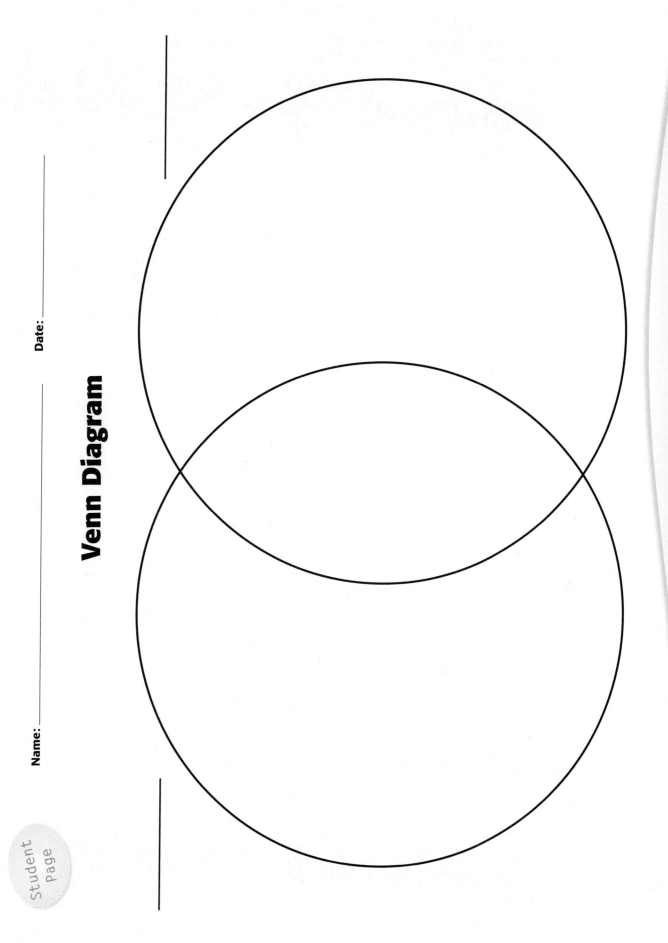

Chapter Ten

Integrating Additional Text Features

I want that book!" said Sarah.

"No, I want it!" replied Rachel.

Two children seemed to be arguing over the same book in the reading area. I walked over to Sarah and Rachel only to notice that both students wanted to read Goldilocks and the Three Bears. I told the children that it wasn't a problem because, luckily, in our classroom we have a basket of books called fairy tales. Inside the box, there *are many copies of the same story. I pulled out another copy of* Goldilocks *and handed it to Sarah. Sarah looked at me and said, "That's not the same book." She was right. It didn't look like the same book. It had a completely different cover than the other book. In fact, there was nothing on the cover except for a green background and a title written in gold letters.*

Sarah's observations of the book's cover, including her attention to the different style/size/color of the title treatment and conclusion that it was a different story, led the way to a mini-lesson on titles and types of print. It was clearly time to investigate how to use titles to predict story content!

There are many such moments during a school day in which the significance of small features in books arises—the importance to readers of titles, different type treatments, and other physical features of the text. Many of these features are difficult to plan a whole lesson around but are more appropriately taught in a moment or integrated into other lessons.

Mini-Lesson: Titles

In order for children to select appropriate books, they need to have practice with reading titles and making connections to topics and main ideas. Writing their own titles provides further practice with attending to key words.

1. Select three or four headlines from newspapers or magazines. Read each title aloud and make predictions about the content of the article. Discuss key words in each title and how they inform readers about content. Point out how each title hooks readers and keeps them reading.

2. Repeat with new headlines. This time let children predict the content. Read one of the articles (or a couple of short ones) to let children check their predictions. Together, point out key words and discuss how the titles hook readers.

3. Continue by letting children practice writing titles. Choose three photographs that could have a variety of titles and meanings. Display one photograph at a time and have children suggest titles for it. What words are important to include? What content would these words signify if an article went with the photograph?

4. To provide further practice, leave several numbered photographs on display with a simple recording sheet. Allow children time to select pictures that interest them and add suggested titles to the list. Be sure to do a group share so that all children can learn from each other and go on to create great titles for their own writing.

Mini-Lesson: Print Styles

The title and print style on the cover of a book make a big statement about what is inside.

1. Display several books that have different print styles on the cover. Ask students what they notice about the titles. Some may have block letters and some shadows. Some may have rainbow colors and others one color. Some may take up most of the space on the cover, while others may look like they're part of the background.

2. Tell students that they will be designing a special title for a piece of writing they've completed. For example, students can design a title for the time line they made (page 68).

3. Have students create three different title "treatments" (or fonts) on a sheet of paper. Point out that they will use the same words in each title but will change the way each title looks. Let students choose and cut out one of their titles to display with their time lines. Invite them to explain their title selection and choice of print styles, size, and so on.

Mini-Lesson: Sidebars

Sidebars appear in many books. Use this activity to help students recognize and understand the purpose of these text features when they read, and to use them in their own writing. Since it can be difficult for children to understand the difference between a caption and sidebar, begin by distinguishing between the two.

1. Review with students what a caption is: A caption is the text that is written to explain a diagram or photograph. It is often located beneath the picture. A caption gives a reader specific information about the picture that is not included in the text. Take a picture walk through a familiar nonfiction book and let students locate examples of captions.

2. Explain that a sidebar is an "extra" piece of information that gives a reader more information about some piece of the topic. A sidebar may or may not have a picture with it.

3. Use several nonfiction books to demonstrate how authors use sidebars. For example, in *Animals You Never Even Heard Of*, by Patricia Curtis (Sierra Club, 1997), the author uses sidebars to give information about the status of 12 rare wild animals, such as the axolotl and the okapi.

4. Further demonstrate the use and purpose of sidebars by adding one to a piece of class writing that has been completed as a whole group. Add a sidebar by using a different-color sheet of paper (trimmed to fit in the margin) and writing something "extra" related to the topic in some way. For example, if the class researched and wrote a report on wildebeests, you might add a sidebar about other animals that live in the African savanna. Glue the sidebar onto the piece of writing. Once your students have practiced several times as a whole group, they will be excited to try this in their own journals, science experiments, or just about anywhere!

Mini-Lesson: An Organizing Framework

As students begin to transition from reading nonfiction to writing nonfiction, it is important to give them a framework for organizing their thoughts. Use the idea of opening and closing sentences and the related details that come in between to help students develop a sense of this structure in the nonfiction they read and write.

1. When reading nonfiction, take time with students to identify opening sentences. Look for key words and ideas that help students predict and make sense of the content that follows. Notice how the details relate to the opening sentence. How does the closing sentence help wrap things up?

2. Help students make a connection to the way they organize information in their own writing by setting up research folders. Glue three library pockets to the inside of a file folder. Label the pockets "Opening Sentence," "Details," and "Closing Sentence."

3. Have students take notes on index cards and then place them in the appropriate pockets.

4. When students are ready to write, they can remove and sequence the cards and then use them to write a paragraph that includes an opening and closing sentence. Students can reuse their folders throughout the year when studying any topic.

Teaching Tip

As your young researchers progress in their understanding of nonfiction, you might also introduce new vocabulary. For example, beginning researchers would refer to the structures as opening and closing sentences while more advanced researchers would use the terms introductory and concluding sentences.

Chapter Eleven

Your Students as Researchers and Writers

Jackson stood tall in front of his classmates and read his research report with pride. He had found the perfect book about horseflies, used his neatest handwriting to write his facts, carefully selected three large and colorful pictures to share with the class, practiced reading the words he had written, and was now using a strong and clear voice to share his information. His audience was listening intently. Upon finishing, Jackson invited the class to ask questions or share comments.

Connor was interested but a little confused. "What does it mean when you said that part about the horseflies' eyes?"

Jackson went back to his paper and quickly found the sentence. "The tiny segments of a horsefly's eyes help it detect predators quickly," he read. "I know right where I got it from. See? Here it is on page 32."

He was totally correct, yet he had no idea what the words meant or how to explain the information to his audience. Clearly, we were ready for a class lesson on paraphrasing!

As students learn how to make sense of the various features of nonfiction they encounter in their reading, they will naturally incorporate some of them into their own writing. As you support students in doing this, take time to work on related skills, including putting information they gather into their own words.

Introduce: What Is Paraphrasing?

Paraphrasing is the act of putting something written or spoken into different words having the same meaning. A general strategy for teaching young readers how to paraphrase is to guide them to use the meaning of the passage to help them decode an unfamiliar word. In thinking about the meaning of the text and the unknown word, they will naturally substitute their own words. This strategy is a comfortable link to teaching children to paraphrase when working with nonfiction.

Teacher: [Since we have just finished a lesson about captions, I choose to share information from a caption that will be supported by a picture.] *I was reading this book,* Getting to Know Nature's Children [by Merebeth Switzer; Grolier, 1985], *and I came across this caption. It says, "For such a small and charming animal, a chipmunk can look surprisingly fierce when scolding an intruder." Let me show you the picture that goes with that caption. What do you think that sentence means? What is the author saying?*

[After taking their responses, I continue.] *How did you figure that out? (used the picture, used the rest of the sentence, used what I know about chipmunks . . .) What were the tricky parts to understand? (charming, fierce, scolding an intruder) If you wanted to share that information with a classmate or younger friend, can you think of a simpler way to say it?* [Accept responses, and then explain to students that saying the same information in your own way is called paraphrasing. Continue

Teaching Tip

Make a connection to the retelling and summarizing students do with fiction they read. Putting information in their own words—whether events from a story or facts from reference materials—is one way for readers to check their understanding of important ideas.

with a brief explanation of why this is an important skill.] *It's very important to be able to paraphrase what you are reading because it helps your brain really understand the information. When you can retell the information in your own words, it helps you be better able to share what you have read with others. If you can explain the information simply, then they can easily understand it and learn from what you've learned!*

Teacher: *Let's try a few more together.* [Several examples follow.] *"Sun jellyfish have tentacles over 200 feet long. They drag these poisonous filaments through the water to stun fish, which they then catch and eat."* [from *Biggest, Strongest, Fastest* by Steve Jenkins; Houghton Mifflin, 1995] *"Mount McKinley, in Alaska, is almost 20,000 feet from base to summit."* [from *Hottest, Coldest, Highest, Deepest* by Steve Jenkins; Houghton Mifflin, 1998] *"Any place that receives less than 10 inches of precipitation a year is considered a desert."* [from *Hottest, Coldest, Highest, Deepest* by Steve Jenkins; Houghton Mifflin, 1998]

Extended practice with the whole group is the best model for students to develop understanding of how paraphrasing works. Taking the time to let students play with the words and hear from each other various attempts at paraphrasing will give them the confidence they need to begin rephrasing an author's words on their own. As we end our work together, we remind ourselves that there are lots of different ways to say the same thing. The facts must stay the same, but there is no one right way to rephrase it!

Explore and Discover

After having many opportunities to listen to classmates paraphrase an author's ideas while in the whole-group setting, students may benefit from additional practice with a partner. This can be easily accomplished using any developmentally appropriate nonfiction books (including any of the suggested titles in this book). Have each pair of students select a nonfiction book. Have one student read a page or two (depending on the amount of text on a page) to a partner. The listener then retells or explains what he or she learned from the reading.

Share and Discuss

Once students have had plenty of opportunities to practice paraphrasing, bring them together to discuss what they know about this skill. What tips will help them remember how to paraphrase when they read and write? Record students' comments on chart paper or poster board to display in the classroom. Encourage students to use the chart as a reminder when they are reading, as a way to make sure they understand the information. Have them use the chart when they are writing their own informational text to make sure they are putting what they've learned about a topic in their own words.

What We Know About Paraphrasing

❊ Notice key words. Think about what you already know about these words.

❊ Retell information in your own words.

❊ Facts must stay the same.

❊ Use words that you know and that classmates can easily understand.

Need More Practice?

Another way to provide extra practice is with a set of fact cards. For a starter set, see page 94. To make others, on index cards simply write facts from developmentally appropriate nonfiction books. Make at least five more cards than the number of students in your class. Have students use the cards with partners as described previously with the books. (See Explore and Discover, page 86.) One student chooses a card and reads it aloud to a partner. The listener paraphrases the information and then selects a new card to read. Model the activity first with students, using what you know about key words to put the information in your own words. These fact cards are especially helpful for students who may be overwhelmed or distracted by an entire book.

Presenting the concept of plagiarism, or the idea of copying an author's words as a form of "stealing," may be developmentally inappropriate for your young students. It is, however, important even as young readers to know that researchers must understand what they are reading well enough to explain it to others in their own words.

Teaching Tip

Presenting the concept of plagiarism, or the idea of copying an author's words as a form of "stealing," may be developmentally inappropriate for your young students. It is, however, important even as young readers to know that researchers must understand what they are reading well enough to explain it to others in their own words.

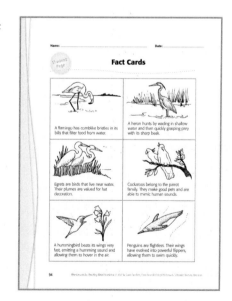

Writing a Nonfiction Book

Researching and writing a nonfiction book is a wonderful way to culminate students' learning and give them a concrete reminder of how to make sense of nonfiction texts. Use the following steps to guide students in focusing on one feature of nonfiction at a time as they complete pages for an information-rich book.

1. Revisit nonfiction books that students are familiar with from a unit of study (for example, books about the rainforest). As you slowly flip through the pages of each book, have students let you know when they spot a familiar feature, such as the contents page, diagrams, captions, maps, a glossary, or a comparison (a text structure). Use this time to review these features with students. If you have class charts on display that summarize information about each feature, review them as well.

2. Read selected passages from some of the books. Let students explain the information in their own words as a way of reviewing what they know about paraphrasing.

3. Give each student a copy of the nonfiction features log (pages 92–93). On their own or with a partner, have students browse the books and record on the log examples they find of different features of nonfiction. They can return to these examples and use them as models when they're ready to create pages for their books.

Teaching Tip

Have children use the log (pages 92–93) to keep track of features of nonfiction they come across in their reading or use in their writing. This will enable you to assess at a glance their understanding of the various features.

4. Give each child a copy of a blank book. (Staple together half or full sheets of copy paper.) Have students write their names at the bottom of the cover (they can return to the cover later to add a title and illustration) and label the first page "Contents." Explain that they will complete the contents page later.

5. Have students choose a favorite feature listed in their logs—for example, a diagram of an anaconda—and use it as a reference to create their own. Explain that students can use the diagram in the book to help with their drawing, but they will need to use what they know about paraphrasing to write labels in their own words. In the case of an anaconda, they might label body parts, diameter, length, characteristic colors and patterns, and so on. Remind students to include a title for their diagram—for example, "All About Anacondas." Suggest that students use a different-color pen to write key words that they will want to include in their glossary.

6. Continue over the next week or so, having students add new information about their topic with each different feature they include (maps, captions, time lines, and so on). Also have students complete the cover and contents page, and add a glossary and index. When students' books are complete, they will have a dynamic collection of information that celebrates their topic of study, as well as a reminder of important features of nonfiction that they will continue to encounter in their own reading.

Teaching Tip

Many curriculum companies offer collections of visually appealing fact cards that are especially helpful for paraphrasing practice. For example, All About Animals Photo Library (Lakeshore Learning) is a collection of 170 photo cards with a colorful picture on one side and a riddle with a few additional lines of information on the reverse. Children will be eager to learn all they can, and can build on the success they experience with explaining the limited text on each card in their own words.

Teaching Connections and Extensions

General wordplay is a logical connection to paraphrasing. Teaching synonyms, antonyms, homonyms, and even contractions blends nicely with the concept of using words to express your ideas clearly, smoothly, and with a particular audience in mind.

Shades of Meaning: Using paint sample cards from a paint store, write a word on the first color and then challenge students to write a synonym for that word on each of the remaining shades—for example, *run, scurry, scamper, sprint, dash*. As a variation, use paint sample cards for practice with antonyms, homonyms, and contractions.

Morning Meeting Game: This is a great game to play during morning meeting or anytime you have a few extra minutes. Gather students in a circle. Choose a word, such as *fuzzy*. Ask the child next to you to think of a synonym for the word—for example, *furry*. Continue around the circle until children are unable to think of another word.

Nonfiction Books to Use With This Lesson

Title	Author/Publisher	Page
Animals		
Actual Size	Steve Jenkins (Houghton Mifflin, 2004)	70
Amazing Animal Facts	Jacqui Bailey, Joe Elliot, and Jayne Miller (Dorling Kindersley, 2003)	15
Animal Homes	Tammy Everts and Bobbie Kalman (Crabtree, 1994)	62
The Best Book of Bugs	Claire Llewellyn (Kingfisher, 1998)	23, 62
Biggest, Strongest, Fastest	Steve Jenkins (Houghton Mifflin, 1995)	15
Bugs	Nancy Winslow Parker and Joan Richards (Mulberry, 1987)	31
Endangered Animals	Lynn M. Stone (Children's Press, 1984)	23
Explore and Discover Reptiles	Claire Llewellyn (Kingfisher, 2002)	39
Eye Wonder: Ocean	Samantha Gray (Dorling Kindersley, 2001)	39
Getting to Know Nature's Children	Merebeth Switzer (Grolier, 1985)	23
The Magic School Bus: In the Time of the Dinosaurs	Joanna Cole (Scholastic, 1994)	70
One Small Square: Backyard	Donald M. Silver (Freeman, 1991)	39
Piglets	Kelly Doudna (ABDO Publishing, 1999)	23
Surprising Sharks	Nicola Davies (Candlewick Press, 2003)	31, 78
Waiting for Wings	Lois Ehlert (Harcourt, 2001)	15
Where Did the Butterfly Get Its Name?	Melvin and Gilda Berger (Scholastic, 2003)	23
Habitats		
Animal Homes	Tammy Everts and Bobbie Kalman (Crabtree, 1994)	62
Eye Wonder: Ocean	Samantha Gray (Dorling Kindersley, 2001)	39
One Small Square: Backyard	Donald M. Silver (Freeman, 1991)	39
Scholastic Atlas of Oceans	Donna Vekteris (Scholastic, 2004)	56, 62
Human Body/Health		
I Wonder Why I Blink and Other Questions About My Body	Brigid Airson (Kingfisher, 1993)	31, 39
The Magic School Bus: Inside the Human Body	Joanna Cole (Scholastic, 1989)	39, 46
Usborne Internet-Linked First Encyclopedia of the Human Body	Fiona Chandler (Usborne, 2004)	23, 62
People		
Fannie in the Kitchen	Deborah Hopkinson (Simon & Schuster, 2001)	70
Let Freedom Ring: Benedict Arnold	Susan R. Gregson (Bridgestone Books, 2002)	70
Martin's Big Words	Doreen Rappaport (Hyperion, 2001)	15

Mini-Lessons for Teaching About Nonfiction

Title	Author/Publisher	Page
People		
A Picture Book of … Series	David A. Adler (Scholastic, 1998)	70
Shake, Rattle & Roll	Holly George (Houghton Mifflin, 2001)	70
Time for Kids Biographies	(HarperCollins, 2006)	70
We the People: The Underground Railroad	Ann Heinrichs (Compass Point Books, 2001)	39
Who Was Johnny Appleseed?	Joan Holub (Grosset & Dunlap, 2005)	70
Places		
A Bird's-Eye View	Marcia S. Freeman (Rand McNally, 1999)	56
Hottest, Coldest, Highest, Deepest	Steve Jenkins (Houghton Mifflin, 1998)	78
Houses and Homes (Around the World Series)	Ann Morris (Lothrop, Lee and Shepard, 1992)	15
Junior Classroom Atlas	(Rand McNally, 2001)	56
Map Keys	Rebecca Aberg (Scholastic, 2003)	56
National Geographic Big Book of Maps	(National Geographic Society, 2001)	56
Primary Atlas	(Rand McNally, 2002)	56
Scholastic Atlas of Oceans	Donna Vekteris (Scholastic, 2004)	56, 62
This Land Is Your Land	Woody Guthrie (Little, Brown, 1998)	15
Types of Maps	Mary Dodson Wade (Scholastic, 2003)	56
Wake Up World! A Day in the Life of Children Around the World	Beatrice Hollyer (Henry Holt, 1999)	15
Plants		
Tell Me Tree: All About Trees for Kids	Gail Gibbons (Little, Brown, 2002)	15
Weather		
Can It Rain Cats and Dogs?	Melvin and Gilda Berger (Scholastic, 1999)	31
Discovering El Niño	Patricia Seibert (Millbrook Press, 1999)	56
Hottest, Coldest, Highest, Deepest	Steve Jenkins (Houghton Mifflin, 1998)	78
The Reasons for Seasons	Gail Gibbons (Holiday House, 1995)	31
Thunderstorms and Lightning	Dean Galiano (Rosen Publishing Group, 2003)	23
Other		
Emergency!	Gail Gibbons (Scholastic, 1994)	70
Look at My Book: How Kids Can Write and Illustrate Terrific Books	Loreen Leedy (Holiday House, 2004)	46
Millions to Measure	David M. Schwartz (HarperCollins, 2003)	46, 78
The Post Office Book: Mail and How It Moves	Gail Gibbons (Thomas Y. Crowell, 1982)	15
Scholastic Atlas of Space	Kenneth Wright (Scholastic, 2004)	39
Throw Your Tooth on the Roof: Tooth Traditions From Around the World	Selby Beeler (Houghton Mifflin, 2001)	15
26 Things Small Hands Do	Coleen Paratore (Free Spirit Publishing, 2004)	39

Name: _____   Date: _____

Features of Nonfiction Log: Part 1

Feature	Book Title/Author	Page	Comments
Contents Page			
Index			
Diagram			
Caption			
Speech Bubble			

Mini-Lessons for Teaching About Nonfiction © 2007 by Diane Farnham, Paula Jensvold & Brigid Kulhowvick, Scholastic Teaching Resources

Features of Nonfiction Log: Part 2

Feature	Book Title/ Author	Page	Comments
Map			
Glossary			
Time Line			
Comparison			

Fact Cards

A flamingo has comblike bristles in its bills that filter food from water.

A heron hunts by wading in shallow water and then quickly grasping prey with its sharp beak.

Egrets are birds that live near water. Their plumes are valued for hat decoration.

Cockatoos belong to the parrot family. They make good pets and are able to mimic human sounds.

A hummingbird beats its wings very fast, emitting a humming sound and allowing it to hover in the air.

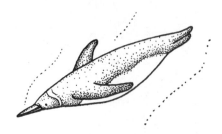

Penguins are flightless. Their wings have evolved into powerful flippers, allowing them to swim quickly.

It's a beautiful June morning, the kind of day that begs for an extra-long recess. Summer vacation is just around the corner. Who can pass up the sunshine? As we are filing back into our classroom, John is carrying a bug box.

"I wonder what kind of bug this is," he says.

"Hey, I saw a diagram of a bug like that in one of our insect books. I'll try to find it," offers Sam.

As soon as we enter the classroom, the two rush to our collection of nonfiction books to research the bug. Sam locates the diagram and they read the caption.

"Look, we found out our bug is a water beetle!" they report excitedly. "Can we research water beetles to find out what they eat?" John and Sam don't wait for my answer. They've already flipped to the index and are scanning the Ws for water beetles. Researching is what we do! I smile, satisfied with how far my students have come this year and knowing that they are just beginning. There is so much to learn.

As I sit back and watch my young researchers, I am pleased. Whereas in September my students looked to me as a resource for acquiring new information, they are now independently able to access information by reading nonfiction text. From reading a contents page and using alphabetizing skills to access information in an index to identifying parts of a diagram and using a glossary to pronounce and understand important words, I know that they have acquired many of the tools they need to grow as successful and confident learners.

Notes